MODERN MARRIAGE

THE MACMILLAN COMPANY
NEW YORK · BOSTON · CHICAGO · DALLAS
ATLANTA · SAN FRANCISCO

MACMILLAN AND CO., Limited
LONDON · BOMBAY · CALCUTTA · MADRAS
MELBOURNE

THE MACMILLAN COMPANY
OF CANADA, Limited
TORONTO

MODERN MARRIAGE

A HANDBOOK FOR MEN

by

PAUL POPENOE

*General Director, the American Institute of Family Relations,
Los Angeles, Calif.*

Lecturer in Biology, University of Southern California

Second Edition

NEW YORK

THE MACMILLAN COMPANY

1943

173.1

P81m

19859

Feb, 1944

MODERN MARRIAGE

PREFACE TO THE SECOND EDITION

EDUCATION for marriage has made remarkable advances since the first publication of this book in 1925, and the amount of new material now available has led me to re-write it entirely. I have, however, adhered to the plan of a popular handbook for men and have not tried to include technical discussions of many points that really deserve fuller treatment. For the benefit of those who want to verify statements or locate additional information, I have given some references to other publications in which I have presented the data more extensively. I have also added references to a number of other recent and valuable studies in this field. These are grouped as Appendix VIII and are referred to by superior numbers throughout the text. Through these anyone will be able to get abundant citations and reading lists for further study.

For illustrative material I have drawn upon observations in many parts of the United States during the past quarter of a century, always altering details beyond recognition. Of course all names are fictitious.

Like every other author, I am indebted to innumerable friends. I want particularly to mention the staff members, past and present, of the American Institute of Family Relations; hundreds of former students scattered through almost every state in the union; and my brother, Dr. Herbert Popenoe.

P. P.

June, 1940.

FROM THE PREFACE TO THE FIRST EDITION

Purpose

THAT something is wrong with marriage today is universally admitted and deplored. The number of celibates, of mismated couples, of divorces, of childless homes, of wife deserters, of mental and nervous wrecks; the frequency of marital discord, of prostitution and adultery, of perversions, of juvenile delinquency, tells the story. The commonest tendency of those trying to remedy these difficulties is to attack the framework of monogamy and attempt to break it apart.

2 To aim at the results, instead of at the causes, of an evil is thoroughly in accord with society's customary method of handling difficult problems; it is also thoroughly inefficient, unscientific, and unsuccessful. The evils can be corrected only by removing the causes, not by tinkering with the consequences. The first necessity is to recognize that the primary causes are to be found not in the field of law, or theology, or esthetics, or superstition, not even of economics, but in the field of biology. Man is first of all an animal; mating and reproduction are first of all (though much else of importance has been added to them) functions of the animal; and biology must have the first—not necessarily the last or only—word regarding any problem that concerns them.

This book is, therefore, written from the biological point of view. It takes man as it finds him, and tries to make clear how he can fit himself into the American civilization of the twentieth century in such a way as to provide for his own greatest satisfaction and the progressive evolution of the race. These two aims must go together.

The trouble with marriage today is not, as some have supposed, that the fundamental principle of monogamy no longer accords with human nature. My thesis is that this principle is at the present time scientifically unassailable. The real trouble is highly complex, but the following aspects of it particularly require consideration:

1. Young people are not properly educated for marriage. Many of them scarcely know what marriage means.

2. They do not always have the guidance to choose mates wisely.

3. They do not understand how to conserve and foster that mutual love which is universally admitted to be the essential element of a happy marriage.

There is available in modern science a large body of facts bearing on these points—enough to clear up most of the problems that arise. It would be far beyond the bounds of a single book to include all the existing data; but I have tried here to make at least the most directly applicable part of the information accessible, in the belief that it will be of value to men who are high enough in the evolutionary scale to let reason, along with instinct and emotion, play an appropriate part in directing their lives.

P. P.

February, 1925.

CONTENTS

CONTENTS

CONTENTS

CHAPTER I

ARE YOU OLD ENOUGH TO MARRY?

MARRIAGE is an enterprise for grown-ups—perhaps the most serious of all adult responsibilities.

One of the main reasons for failure in marriage is that people who have not grown up try to make a child's game out of it.

These people may be fully grown, physically. A man may be 6 feet tall, 30 years old, weigh 180 pounds; but in his emotional and social development he may be no more than six years old or even six months old. He is not ready for marriage!

If you are thinking at all about marriage, begin by asking yourself whether you are really old enough to marry. Check over the stages of your own development—have you gone through all of them? Start at the zero hour, with a newborn baby:

1. *The infant loves himself.* He is wholly self-centered. He is concerned only with the gratification of his own desires, the satisfaction of his own needs—or whims. If he does not get what he wants, he will have a tantrum.

He does not care who suffers, provided he gets his own way. His parents have perhaps been working hard all day. After dinner they change their clothes, and then go out and dance till midnight. They return dead tired and badly in need of a little sleep so that they can repeat the performance next day. That makes no difference to the baby. He will not hesitate to get them out of bed at 3 A.M., and to keep them up all the rest of the night, if he wants a little nourishment or merely a little sociability.

He wants what he wants when he wants it.

"You can't blame him," people say. "He's just a baby. It's natural for babies to behave that way."

Unfortunately, many a man has never progressed beyond that stage. He can love only himself; his one thought is the gratification of his own whims; and if he does not get his way he will promptly have a tantrum, just as he did when he was still drawing his nourishment from the maternal breast.

2. *Normally, however, the child's horizon expands in a few years to take in his parents,* particularly his mother (or her substitute). He then loves her as well as himself; his love-life now turns on an axis suspended between himself and his mother.

This is natural and desirable for a six-year-old. If at the age of thirty-six he has not progressed beyond this, if he still can see nothing in the world more important than himself and his mother, then his development has been arrested prematurely.

Such a man is likely never to marry. He is, unconsciously, so deeply in love with his mother that it seems disloyal to put any other woman in her place. He is always talking about how wonderful marriage is; he is anxious to marry just as soon as he finds the right girl; but he never finds the right girl! This mother fixation probably accounts for more old bachelors among otherwise superior men than any other one thing.

If he does marry, his wife is likely to have a hard time. She thought she was getting a husband at the altar, but she finds she obtained only an oversized child to "mother" and nurse. If his real mother is still living, he is continually turning to her with his confidences rather than to his wife. The latter's position often becomes tragic.

3. *Normally, again, the boy expands his interests in a few years to include his "gang"*, a group of persons of his own age and own sex. His concerns are no longer exclusively in the home; he is beginning to look to outsiders for his scale of values.

In the development of the emotional life, it is important to note that one does not leave a stage behind to enter another, as the caterpillar leaves his chrysalis behind when he emerges as a butterfly. It is merely a question of enlarging the area covered. When one throws a stone into a pond, the circles become wider and wider; but the center, the point where the stone landed, is still there. That point is yourself. A man never ceases to love himself. If he does, he is insane, literally. What happens normally is that his horizon broadens so that Self forms relatively a smaller and smaller part of the whole. There is a change of perspective with each year.

So the boy in his pre-adolescent years gets out of the

home and learns how to get along with his equals. He is becoming socialized.

So long as his concern is mainly with his parents, he cannot learn to deal with equals. His parents may give him the best of it; they may give him the worst of it; but one thing is certain, they cannot treat him as an equal. If he is going to get along in the world, however, he must learn how to get along with those on a level with himself. He gets the most important lessons in this art at the gang age.

4. *A few years later, in the high school or the college period, he begins to take more active interest in the other sex.*

At first this is a generalized interest. He is interested in all girls just because they are girls. Little by little during the ensuing years his attention is focused for longer and longer periods of time on one girl. He will go with one for a whole semester. Next year he goes with another. In college he may even become engaged to one. Thus, by a process of trial and error, he is learning about girls, is learning about himself with reference to girls.

5. *Finally, he selects one as a life-long partner;* and he has then grown up emotionally. He has reached the level of monogamy, which represents adult attainment.

Unfortunately, it is all too easy for a man to be held up at some point before he reaches the adult level.

Many men, as already said, have really never outgrown the infantile stage of self-love. They are old enough to qualify legally for a marriage license; but their love-life stopped short at the infantile level. They are not old enough to marry.

Others have never emancipated themselves from exclusive dependence on their mothers: they are still tied to apron strings; emotionally, they have not been weaned. They are not old enough to marry.

Still others never outgrow the gang age. They are afraid of girls. They may be fifty years old; but spiritually, so to speak, they are still nothing more than Boy Scouts. They become old bachelors, woman-fearers— and perhaps, to cover up their feeling of insecurity, woman-haters. They are not old enough to marry.

A large part of the population has never passed beyond the adolescent stage of finding one member of the other sex about as attractive as another. They are not old enough to marry.

No man can skip a stage in this process of growing up emotionally. Suppose, for instance, that he misses the gang age. He has never learned the give-and-take of association with equals. He goes into high school or college and wants romantic friendships with girls. But, because he has never learned to deal with equals, he cannot associate with these girls on a basis of equality. There are only two kinds of love in his make-up; namely, self-love and mother-love. All that he can offer a girl is the opportunity to mother him.

Needless to say, girls are subject to arrests of development in this way just as are boys. In fact, infantilism is perhaps commoner among girls, though certainly more offensive among boys. A girl who is cute and kittenish may find admirers; a man who is cute and kittenish will be admired only by himself.

Emotional maturity, therefore, is a prerequisite to successful marriage; and the man who has not grown up must begin by analyzing his own personality and then getting a broader and more normal social life to bring him up to par.[127] *

In comparison with emotional maturity, other forms of maturity are of minor importance. Child marriages are, of course, objectionable. The 1930 federal census enumerated 824 males and 4,506 females who were fourteen years old or less, and who were married, widowed, or divorced. Everyone denounces such marriages; but it would be even more profitable to denounce the vastly more numerous marriages in which the partners are able to vote but intellectually have the minds of children—imbeciles who perhaps have less real intelligence than an average child in the first grade at school. The "child bride" may grow up some day; the imbecile bride never will! However, the happiness or unhappiness of a marriage is determined more by the emotional age than by the physical or the intellectual age.

The Time to Marry Is When You Have Found the Right Girl.

After you have grown up emotionally, the time to marry is when you have found the right girl; and after

* Superior numbers appearing throughout the book refer to Appendix VIII, List of References.

you have found her, every day of delay is merely a day that you have lost from your life and cannot replace. In practice, many men go about this search for the right girl in much the same frame of mind in which they buy a new suit of clothes.

You have known for a long time that you must some day get a new suit; but you do not pay much attention to the matter—it is in the back of your mind. You may come to it gradually; or you may make a sudden decision. You may finally go to the clothier's because you have been working up to the point for months and saving your money accordingly; or something may precipitate the action—criticism of your old suit, an invitation to a place where you want to look your best, or an accident to your present garments.

Whatever the reason, there comes a day when you say to yourself, "I can't put it off any longer"; and you go down town, determined to come home with a new suit. The need that you have long recognized has at last translated itself into action.

Then you shop around a little—unless you are so inexperienced, so easy to please, or so lacking in sales-resistance that you take the first suit that is offered to you persuasively.

When at last you make a decision, you take the best you can afford of those that appeal to you. If you are badly in need of a suit, and the market is low, you may not have much choice; but you have to make a decision, nevertheless. On the other hand, you know that if you could afford to pay more money, you could get a suit that you would like better; but the hundred-dollar suit in the window is simply out of your class—you could not live up to it; and you do not feel any great chagrin over having to take a $35 suit—that price represents your level.

This illustration (not very flattering, perhaps to feminine self-esteem; but girls themselves often go about marrying in the same way) could be pushed farther; but I think the point is clear. When you buy a suit, it is because you are ready to buy one. A year earlier you would not have been interested; you were not in the market. A year later it is no use to offer you a suit; you already have one.

The time of marriage is often determined in much the same way—by your own readiness, your own feeling of an unfilled need. If this feeling is on an adult level, then you have reached the right age to marry. That is the age at which marriage is most likely to result in happiness.

Normally, this time arrives in the early twenties. Some men (and more women, because they mature earlier) are ready a few years before that; but the need to finish education, to get a job, interferes with matrimony. They will not marry as early as they want to. This may be no loss: they may not be ready for marriage at an adult level; they may be seeking merely a mother substitute, or a sanction for sexual relations that represent no more than infantile and adolescent desires.

It is sometimes alleged that the time of marriage is determined mainly by economic readiness, and much is said of the number of young people who have long since been ready to marry but cannot afford the step. I shall say more about this in Chapter XIV; but just now a moment's consideration will reveal that the financial situation is often only a part of the broader background. If two young people are emotionally ready for marriage, they will probably head for the License Bureau, whether they can afford it or not. (This does not deny, of course, that many couples borrow $2.00 for a license when they are not prepared emotionally for marriage.) If, on the other hand, two young people are not emotionally prepared to marry, they can easily explain that they are held back by financial hindrances, even though they are relatively "well fixed."

A newspaper survey that was said to represent the answers of 10,000 unmarried women revealed that, among those between eighteen and twenty years of age, 50 per cent said they were unmarried because the "boy friend" could not afford to marry. I think anyone with a slight knowledge of adolescence will recognize that in many instances this was merely a rationalization, just as was the answer of another 17 per cent in this age group—that they had not married because they were "career women." Everyone is acquainted with some of these eighteen-year-old career women!

Finances are an important part of the whole story, but the determination of bride and groom is what pulls the trigger.

The average age at first marriage for native whites in the United States is twenty-five for men and twenty-two for women; and while a year or two less might be desirable, this average seems to work out pretty well. The actual age at marriage is not what determines the happiness in marriage; happiness can be attained at any age if you are ready for it.

The man who marries at the normal time (in the early twenties) has many advantages,[57] so well recognized that it is not necessary to do more than enumerate them: he gets *more* happiness, because it begins earlier; he leads a more healthful life, physically, mentally, and emotionally, and is therefore likely to live longer; he is likely to have more children, to be a better companion for them, and to have a longer period of time to be with them.

The man's age also determines his wife's age, to some extent, because he tends to marry a girl a few years younger than himself, as the census figures show. As he marries later, the spread between his age and that of his wife tends to increase:[9] while the average man of twenty-five marries a woman of twenty-two, the average man of thirty-five marries a woman, not of thirty-two, but of twenty-seven or twenty-eight. This difference is the source of disaster to many educated girls who delay marriage and find when they come to look for a husband, that there are none to be had, because the men of their own age are marrying younger girls, and the older men who are statistically likely to marry them are already married.

However, 10 per cent of all men marry girls of their own age. This tendency seems to have increased during the depression, and is always common in college matches because they are so often between classmates.[44] Another 10 per cent of men marry women who are older than themselves (although only one wife out of every thirty-five is more than two years older than her husband [20]); the remaining 80 per cent marry girls who are younger. Here again there is no marked difference in happiness, because each gets most frequently the kind of wife he wanted. Some of our California data[108] showed unusually happy husbands who had married women twelve years younger than themselves—although there were only a few of them. Mr. N., a diffident and bookish lawyer, married a widow twenty-one years older than himself. He needed someone to take care of him, and Mrs. N. found great satisfaction in the job. It was one of the happiest marriages I have ever encountered, and her death left him quite at sea. Some other man might not have been suited in this partnership; but some other man did not have to be. It was Mr. N.'s marriage, and it suited him.

People Marry Nowadays Earlier
Than They Used to.

One of the most widespread errors in the discussion of marriage is the idea that people nowadays marry later in life than their parents and grandparents did. This is so firmly believed, and repeated by so many respectable authorities, that it is hard to convince anyone of the error; yet it is false. If anything, the average age of marriage is lower now than it was half a century ago. In fact there are at this moment in the United States some 600,000 marriages in which the bride was under sixteen;[27] and in a single year there were 3,153 *births* to mothers who were fourteen or less at the time.

Increasing education has probably delayed the marriage of the small part of the population which gets higher education (and, in the case of women, has often led to failure to marry at all). So much of the discussion centers on these educated people that one may forget they are only a small part of the entire population. The following comparison of post-war averages will illustrate this:

MEDIAN AGE AT FIRST MARRIAGE	YEARS
All California women	21.6
Women college graduates	26
Married women in *Who's Who*	29

But for the bulk of the population the trend has been the other way: not only have people tended to marry at earlier ages but fewer of them have remained unmarried than was the case half a century or more ago.

Marriage and divorce alike are markedly affected by business conditions.[111] In hard times marriages decline, and divorces decline still more. In flush times marriages increase, and divorces increase still more in proportion.[116] During a war there is usually a decrease in the number of marriages, followed by a sharp jump in the rate after peace is declared.[119] All such factors cause fluctuations in the marriage curve. In the decade following 1930 there appears to have been a slight tendency toward delayed marriage. In general, however, census figures show no broad trend toward delayed marriages in the last few generations—no matter who tells you the contrary.[46]

It is also widely alleged that early marriages are not so likely to be happy. This is one of those glib generalizations that is passed around solemnly until it comes to be taken as gospel truth. There is no real basis for it, when one comes to study the record.[60] Available data suggest a slight increase in divorce among couples married before the age of twenty—but what would one expect? What kind of people marry in their teens? Often young people who have little education and do not expect to get much more. And the group includes also many marriages in which one party—perhaps the girl—was marrying mainly to get away from home restraint. It includes a lot of immature, runaway marriages of impulsive young people lacking in self-control and foresight. It likewise includes "shotgun marriages" brought about by the unexpected pregnancy of the girl. All such marriages start with a handicap; so one would not expect them to turn out as well as marriages between mature persons with more feeling of responsibility, who are marrying deliberately after due preparation.

The group of early marriages therefore necessarily includes some that are more or less predestined to turn out badly; and they lower the average. Even at that, the early marriages make a pretty good showing; and it is important to recognize the correct interpretation of the divorce figures. Emil and Martha, a foolish young couple, let themselves in for a forced marriage, in the third year of high school, and were never happy. That is not surprising. But their unhappiness does not mean that if Horace and Alice, who married successfully at the age of thirty, had married ten years earlier, they would have been any less happy than they are. They might have been just as happy, or more so, and they might in that way have had ten years more of happiness in their lives.

In short, the important factor is the quality of the people who are marrying, not their age.*

If one sought a broad formula, he might decide that people should marry after they are physically mature, after they are emotionally mature, and before they are intellectually mature. The desirability of physical and emotional maturity hardly requires discussion. It is also obvious, I think, that after a man has stopped growing intellectually, the difficulties of adjustment may be

---

* One study,[32] which has been widely quoted, was made on couples who appeared in the Philadelphia Court of Domestic Relations. This is probably not the best place to investigate the point; but in any event, the findings of this study are contradicted by another study[47] made in the same court. The most recent study[11] quoted in favor of late marriage was made on 526 couples in or near Chicago. Of these, 105 represented graduate students who were apparently well prepared for marriage, and very successful in it, at least during the first few years (the average length of marriage of the 526 couples was only three years). People who had done graduate or professional work and who married late are not representative of the entire population. One familiar with modern society would expect them to be happier than many others in marriage. The large number of them in this particular study may have overweighted it and naturally colored the findings. What this particular (and in general, very valuable) study really demonstrates, perhaps, is that if one examines couples who married late and were happy, one will conclude that late happiness and marriage are associated! Other studies[108] show how unjustifiable it is to suppose that an early marriage is necessarily handicapped in any way.

greater. He will then be set in his ways, perhaps living in a rut.

When two people marry while they are still in a plastic stage, they may grow together, or they may grow apart. It is for them to decide which way they will grow! It is often argued that people should marry after their personalities are fully formed; it can then be known whether they are congruous. This argument represents a widespread and objectionable concept of marital adjustment. It is almost impossible to get some people to recognize the fact that compatibility is a *product* of intelligent marriage, not something ready-made which either does or does not exist. Successful husbands and wives have more interests in common after ten or twenty years than they did when they first married— naturally. They have cultivated interests in common.* Unsuccessful marriages have gone awry, often because the partners made no real effort to travel in the same direction.

A moment's analysis will show how specious is the argument that if you marry a young woman you may find after a while that she has not grown in the direction you desired. This does happen all too often, partly because the couple do not try hard enough to grow together, partly because each may have a preformed idea of the direction in which the other must grow. But such

---

* If they are intelligent, they will also have broadened and enriched their lives by cultivating many interests that are not in common. After 10 or 20 years of marriage they should have more interests of both kinds.

difficulties are not inherent in successful marriages; they are inherent in unsuccessful personalities.

People differ widely in their attainment of maturity in these various ways. Generally speaking, men will be physically mature in the early twenties, women a little sooner. From a strictly physical point of view, child-bearing is easier for a girl in her teens than at any other time.[31] This is not an argument for child marriage; merely a reminder that delayed childbearing cannot be justified as for the good of either mother or child. Emotionally, men and women should be mature in their early twenties—women, again, maturing more rapidly; but there is much greater variation here, since so many people remain indefinitely at one stage or another of arrested development. Intellectually, the largest part of one's development has occurred before the voting age; thereafter it tapers off slowly.

From every point of view, then, the early twenties appear to be the preferable time for marriage; but never forget that matter of emotional maturity! Marriage cannot be made into a game for children to play success-fully—even if those children are thirty or forty years old.

CHAPTER II

WHAT KIND OF WIFE DO YOU WANT?

SIMILARITY is the general basis of choice in marriage. Men tend to select brides who, more than the average, resemble themselves in almost every respect one can imagine. They tend to wed girls who have a somewhat similar social background, and similar intelligence,[38] health, and tastes.

In fact, it is hard to find any traits in which similarity is not the rule. Two exceptions come to mind: red hair and bad temper. It is seldom that one finds husband and wife both red-headed; while one explosive temper in the family appears to be all that can be tolerated. But with trivial exceptions of that sort, the general rule of similarity holds good, and for obvious reasons; namely, that people who have a good deal in common—who speak the same language, have the same habits of life, attend the same church, and enjoy the same friends and recreations —are more likely to meet each other and to be congenial after they meet than are those who differ markedly in background, in tastes, in philosophy of life.[102]

The similarity that exists between husband and wife is therefore largely a by-product of similarity of backgrounds; and it is not necessary to seek too anxiously for identity of interests—in fact, such identity (if it could

17

exist) might be monotonous. Commenting on the famous friendship of two English liberal statesmen, Richard Cobden and John Bright, a biographer has remarked that they were enough alike for harmony, not enough alike for boredom. That would not be a bad formula for marriage. Everyday observation shows that happy marriages are not produced by identity of interests, but by sympathy with each other's interests, together with a good stock of common tastes and habits in the little matters of daily life or, lacking this, a considerable amount of tolerance and adjustability.

While general similarity is therefore desirable, the really important factor is the attitude toward life. Two people who are determined to make a success of marriage, who regard it as the most important job they will ever tackle, who seek to exhaust all the resources of science to promote it, and who are resolved to let nothing but a catastrophe interfere with their success—such persons will make a success of marriage as they would make a success of almost anything else they tried.

While the average man wants a wife who resembles himself, this does not quite cover intelligence.[98] Studies show that the average man approves, or at least marries, a girl who is a little below him in intelligence and education. This at least is true of the professional, semi-professional, and business groups. In the levels of skilled and unskilled labor, our data indicate that the average man has fewer years of schooling than his wife.

Probably a man feels more sure of himself, more conscious of superiority ("It's not conceit," said the bishop.

"It's just the consciousness of superiority!") when his wife can look up to him. Girls seem to prefer this situation, too. But if men marry girls who are a little below them in educational level, this leaves no one to marry the highly educated girl. Hence she may either fail to marry (in a disastrous proportion of all cases) or may marry someone less educated than herself.[89]

In the latter case, she too often thinks she has married beneath her; she sympathizes with herself because she did not get a better man, and keeps her husband continually on the defensive, sometimes building up in him a serious inferiority complex. Eleanor, for instance, has little to her credit except a diploma, which she got because her parents could afford to, and did, force her through college with the connivance of the registrar. She married Henry, who had to quit college at the end of his Freshman year and help to support the family, because of his father's death. Henry is probably far ahead of his wife in genuine intelligence; he is an outstandingly successful young business man, regarded by the other men of the town as a leader; he is personally attractive and socially minded; but because he is "not a college man" Eleanor tries continually to make him feel inferior. This attitude, which has almost wrecked their marriage, is doubtless based on her own feeling of inferiority—her thought that she has nothing to her credit except a college degree and therefore must make the most of this. One can find plenty of happy marriages in which there is a wide disparity of academic attainment; but before a man marries a girl who has much more schooling than himself, he should make sure that she knows the difference between intelligence and ability on the one hand and years of schooling on the other; that she does not falsely over-value school attainments; in a word, that she has some sense.

With these preliminary remarks, I will touch briefly on some of the characteristics that recent studies show to be most important for a wife:

1. Her Parents Are Happily Married.

Since one's attitude toward life is so decisive of success in marriage, the child from a broken home has often a serious liability in the patterns acquired in earlier years. A man who has grown up in a family where selfishness, intolerance, cruelty, dishonesty, indifference rule, may become so warped that he carries these patterns over into his own marriage later, with disastrous results. Our studies show that where both partners come from happy homes, their chance of success in marriage is nearly half again as great as if they came from unhappy homes.[100]

Faulty family background is therefore a liability to be weighed—not necessarily to be shunned. Sometimes a girl with such a handicap profits by the lesson. Gertrude, for example, came into the Institute of Family Relations for that reason. "I'm going to be married," she said. "All my life I have seen nothing but unhappiness in my own home. For years my first thought has been that when I married, I would move heaven and earth to avoid making the mess of my own life that my parents have made of theirs. I want you to give me everything you can think of that will help me." Gertrude, willing to work twice as hard as anyone else to make her marriage a success, reached her goal; while Henrietta, who had been brought up in a family where everything was so peaceful that she supposed all family life to be like that, was unprepared to make any effort— and failed.

A more deep-seated difficulty is that the members of broken homes are sometimes inferior people in every way (see Chapter VIII), and the offspring is inferior, not so much because of the broken home (which is merely a symptom) but because he comes from inferior stock. Whether you like it or not, you *are* marrying the whole family; and you will therefore do well to look them over. A family of long-lived people is likely to be physically sound and disease-resistant; a family that has been self-supporting is likely to have given its members habits of thrift and good management; a family that is happy and reasonably free from mental disease is likely to be made up of persons who are emotionally stable.

2. She Gets Along Well with Her Own Family.

If she has a good family, but is at outs with it—if she hates her mother and is ashamed of her father—she may adopt the same attitude toward you at some time in the future.

Many a girl feels that her home and family are a drag,

an impediment to her attempts to get a satisfactory husband. Sometimes this is perfectly true. An undesirable home serves to decrease her "bargaining power" in the process of attracting a mate who will meet her requirements. This is a more important process for her than for her future husband, although it is so important for him that it deserves more attention than sometimes is given. He is going to select a wife; she is going to select not only a husband but a standard of living. The whole scale of her existence for the rest of her life will depend on what caliber of man she is able to marry. Since there is normally a good deal of bargain-driving, of attempts to get as good a bargain as possible, going on between two persons who are looking for life-partners (this bargain-driving is nearly always unconscious, and often conscious as well), an intelligent girl will naturally try to make the most of her assets and, unfortunately, sometimes try to conceal her liabilities. If a business man did this in entering a partnership, he would be guilty of fraud and would expose himself to severe penalties. Of course, such a girl also exposes herself to severe penalties; but she will always hope for the best!

A girl, then, cannot be blamed for wanting to rise above her parents, for wanting to make more of a success than they did; that is greatly to her credit. But if she rebels against them with deceit and tantrums, cannot accept emotionally her own parentage or background, cannot face it honestly, she may have defects of personality that will wreck her own home in the future. The girl who has normally affectionate relations with her parents and the other members of her family is a good prospect; and this includes two thirds or more of the girls in the educated part of the population.[11]

3. *She Has Definite Interests in Life.*

The girl who "has nothing on her mind" except to "get a man" is likely to have still less on her mind after she gets her man. Much of the unnecessary trouble in married life grows out of the fact that the wife resents what she has to do (that is, her share of the management of the home and children), but has no other interests. Schools have failed to give some young women any abiding and satisfying interests; such girls naturally have little recreation except to sympathize with themselves and seek sympathy from others. A proper education [70] would prepare girls to get more satisfaction from home-making (after all, it is much more in accord with their traditional and fundamental tendencies than is the work which most men do in the world in accordance with traditional and fundamental masculine tendencies). It would provide them with ample understanding of how they can draw on the resources of the community and in turn contribute to it, along with home-making. Finally, it would prepare them in advance to fill their lives with richly satisfying activity after their children are "up and gone." At present many schools do a great injustice to men by failing to give any understanding of these things to girls. There has been some improvement; but men will still have to protect their own interests by selecting girls who, in spite of their so-called education, have demonstrated that they have mature and efficient personalities. This is evidenced by

(a) *Intellectual interests*. The average man painstakingly avoids a "highbrow" or a girl who makes him unpleasantly conscious of her intellectual superiority. Sometimes he is too sensitive on this point! Many superior girls still pay the penalty of life-long celibacy for the spurious culture which is foisted on them in school and college; they find men are not excited by their monologues on modern music or their attempts to get up a debate on whether one inferior poet is more to be admired than some other inferior poet. But if the man leans over so far backward as to marry a girl with no intellectual interests, he will get little real comradeship out of his marriage. An intelligent and healthy interest in the important things that are going on in the world is an excellent promise of success in marriage.

(b) *Membership in organizations*. A girl, to meet the requirements of her husband, need not necessarily be a community leader. Some of those leaders are, in fact, driven by the "masculine protest" (see Chapter V, page 70) and will find it hard to adjust themselves to a genuinely co-operative marital partnership. But the girl who belongs to no organizations, who takes part in no group activities, is open to suspicion. If she is not popular with her own sex, she may not have grown up even as far as the gang age, which I described in the preceding chapter. If she is either unwilling or unable to co-operate in group activities, she may have stopped short in development somewhere far below the level of adult emotional maturity, which is marked by co-operation. She may have a severe inferiority complex, or be so self-centered that she cannot work with anyone else, is not interested in anyone except herself. In that case, she may well be all the more desperate to get the exclusive attention of some man, in order to bolster up her self-esteem. The girl who has taken a normal part in community affairs through high school or college activities, Sunday school or church work, and through membership in social, philanthropic, recreational, or other organizations, is more likely to have a personality well suited to marriage or to any other adult enterprise—for it must always be remembered that marriage is merely one special form of adult co-operation;[103] that it does not depend on mysterious characteristics which have no relation to other activities; and, conversely, that if one has made a failure in all other adult relationships, this record of incompetence is not likely to be reversed by any peculiar magic involved in a wedding ceremony.

(c) *A job?* What about the working girl? A large part of the educated young women today take jobs after they finish school and before marrying—if they marry at all. What is the effect of such work on their fitness for marriage? The subject has been debated profusely, and it has often been pointed out that the working girl acquires habits of industry and application, learns the value of money, and is better qualified for marriage than one who does nothing but loaf on the front porch reading the Confession magazines.

Studies bear out the conclusion that the girl who has worked is a good marital prospect, certainly much better than her sister who has specialized in Confessions. The job is valuable evidence mainly as an indication of seriousness of purpose, however. Another sister who, while not employed for pay, has been active in community affairs, or who has managed her father's home after the death of the mother, is no less well qualified. Since women teachers are sometimes prone to extol the virtues of pre-marital wage-earning, it may be worth while to point out some possibilities on the other side.

In the first place, girls in business and industry have been trained primarily to compete with men, instead of to co-operate with them. They have been led to believe that they must fight men to get jobs, and then fight men some more to hold these jobs. This is not good training for that co-operation of the two sexes which is the essence of marriage.[103]

In the second place, some girls look on the job not as a "career" but as a necessary evil during the time they are awaiting marriage. They have no consuming interest in the work, whatever it may be; their interest is to get through the day with as little effort as possible, and to get away as early as possible to a good time elsewhere. They learn to watch the clock, to cut the corners, to consider work a nuisance, and to think that the real values of life are to be found only in play. A girl with these ideals is ill equipped for home-making; she is too likely to carry over into her new job the same attitudes, regarding the time she puts in at home as a mere deprivation of fun that is to be had elsewhere. Occasionally she has become so accustomed to the excitement of a job in the midst of a lot of other people—in a department store, for instance—that when she "settles down" at home after marriage, the quiet and isolation are intolerable. She is miserable and, without recognizing the cause, will blame her husband for her unhappiness. The only solution may be to get her out of the home and back into a job.

In the third place, girls with superior jobs, particularly those involving executive activities, have to develop aloof, impersonal attitudes toward men. They cannot hold their positions or get promotion merely by practising a "come hither" look. Thus they antagonize, quite unintentionally, the young men who ought to marry them, and are left unmarried. It is no accident that the two occupations for women in which sex appeal does have a commercial value, namely those of the actress and the stenographer, probably have the highest marriage rates.[98]

The mere fact, then, that a girl has held a job before marriage is no proof that she is well educated for matrimony. Use your own judgment.

4. She Has a "Good Disposition."

For the present purpose this term may be taken as largely synonymous with emotional maturity. The girl who is selfish, demanding, domineering, petulant, snobbish, dishonest, mean in little ways, or given to sulking and pouting or to tantrums, has simply not grown up. Care must be taken, however, not to classify as undesirable traits the characteristics that are merely second nature to women, that are wholly normal to the female, even though not admired by the male sex (see Chapter V).

In general, the girl who has grown up in a good-sized family is likely to have learned how to get along with people, and the "only child" is correspondingly handicapped. Since about one person in every four is now an only child, the problem is a big one. The only child may do as well as other children or even better in the kindergarten or grades; she profits by having had more attention from her parents, is perhaps more aggressive. Her (and his) difficulty shows up later on, in marriage; and this finding has been confirmed by virtually every study of the subject. The only child probably carries a handicap of at least 20 per cent in marriage. This does not mean that an only child cannot succeed in marriage, for most of them do succeed. It means that the only child must recognize this handicap frankly and work a little harder to overcome it than do others. When two persons marry, each of whom is an only child, there is double reason for getting all possible help in advance of marriage, and for constant determination to avoid difficulties that may otherwise appear.

The one who is naturally happy is likely also to be happy in marriage, while the person who has never been happy may have an inability to find happiness anywhere. There are plenty of cases in which a partner with a naturally happy disposition is well satisfied with a marriage which her (or his) own spouse regards a failure.[108]

5. She Should Be Fond of Children.

The woman (or man) who dislikes children is not emotionally normal; and even if the marriage is childless, the partner may pay a heavy penalty in frustration and in having to live with a neurotic mate.

6. She Should Be "Typically Feminine."

This characterization involves many things that have been said already; but the average man feels strongly on the matter, and the statistics seem to justify him.

I asked twenty-five intelligent men to write out their ideas on this subject. Only one of them wanted to marry a woman who was low in femininity. Thirteen of them wanted a wife, or woman friend, to be of average normal development in this respect; eleven wanted her to be on the high side. They emphasized strongly their dislike of the mannish, aggressive female, often coarse and sometimes highly neurotic, who tries to beat them at their own game, to be the feminine equivalent of a "man about town." They emphasized even more strongly their admiration of what they considered "typically feminine" qualities: good grooming, sympathy, gentleness, modesty, grace, refinement, companionability, social intelligence, and responsiveness. Probably the quality last named is as valuable as any other to a girl who wants to attract men.

Studies show that those women who are sexually most normal are the ones who marry earliest;[1] and that those who are classified by their friends as decidedly feminine are happier in marriage than those of the masculine type —many of whom do not marry at all. I have collected particulars (see Appendix I) concerning 1,479 educated * women who had been married for five years or more and who were rated by close friends or relatives who knew them intimately. These judges classified 37 per cent of the women as highly feminine; 46 per cent as average normals; and 17 per cent as low in the traditional feminine characteristics, leaning rather toward masculinity. Of those high in femininity, 69 per cent were considered to be happy in marriage; of the intermediates, 71 per cent; of those low in femininity, only 51 per cent. Here again it must be remarked that even among the women who were somewhat masculine, half were happy; presumably they married men who wanted wives of that sort. But they make a much less satisfactory showing than do those who are nearer to the conventional standard.

A book might easily be written to discuss just what this "conventional standard" includes, whether it is justifiable, whether it is necessary, and whether it might not be changed desirably. In fact, many books have

---

* In the course of this book I shall be forced to refer a good many times to "the educated part of the population"—or words to that effect. This is not because their marriages are more important than others, but because nearly all of the studies on the subject have been made on this class, which may be defined broadly as including persons who have the equivalent of a high school education, or more.

been written on the subject, although most of them contribute little to a solution. The most careful study [110] indicates that educated women are becoming more and more masculinized; but it is possible that a change in this trend is already beginning. In the light of present knowledge, the masculinization of women adds as little to their own happiness as it does to that of their husbands.

Aggressiveness has been identified [110] as the quality which most sharply differentiates the two sexes in America at the present time.[42] The aggressive and dominant female is therefore one who is essentially adopting masculine patterns; [107] and she is correspondingly unhappy in marriage. I have tabulated some thousands of marriages from this point of view.[76] Where the woman was the boss of the family, only 47 per cent of the marriages were happy; where the husband was the head of the household, 61 per cent were happy. A still higher standard, however, was attained in those mature and cooperative marriages that had two heads—that were running on a fifty-fifty basis. Of these, 87 per cent were happy. Once more I must reiterate that some men want a dominant and aggressive wife. If that is the kind they want, that is the kind they ought to get; and they will not have much trouble in getting one. But the deep-seated tendency of men in general to avoid the dominant, aggressive, masculinized female has good statistical support, so far as happiness in marriage is concerned.

In conclusion, the age-old tendency of men to select wives who contrast with them in sexual differentiation but resemble them in other respects seems to be as strong as ever, and to be associated with the best prospects of success in marriage. It is obvious that with this combination the partners have a great deal in common; and, as I pointed out at the beginning of this chapter, much stress is laid on this in modern discussions, although the proposition is often stated negatively—a woman proposes to divorce her husband because, as she says, "We haven't a thing in common." In such a case, what she really means is that they have almost everything under the sun in common, but that there are a few things which they have isolated, magnified, and determined to differ on. One need not to be too much concerned about having everything in common before marriage. If two persons want to build up interests in common, they can always do so. It is not a question of starting with agreement on every possible topic, but of choosing a congenial companion and then deliberately building up mutual interests. Final success, then, is not a matter of what you start with, but of your attitude toward the whole process of living together.

CHAPTER III

WHERE WILL YOU FIND SUCH A PARAGON?

JOSEPH complains that he has no friends. He is popular with the boys, but that is not what he means. He would like to meet more girls.

"It seems awfully hard to meet any decent girls—you know, girls of your own kind," Gilbert laments. "They don't seem to go to the places I do."

So it runs, from the Atlantic to the Pacific, with complaints from girls even more numerous and vigorous than those from boys. Both often lack a normal social life.

Those not familiar with the facts sometimes suppose that young people today have more social life than is good for them. Our studies indicate that this may be true of about 10 per cent of young people of high school and college age; and that about 50 per cent have little or none—less, at any rate, than is desirable.

A study in Minnesota confirmed statistically what everyone knows: that this lack of social contacts is one of the commonest causes of an inferiority complex.[21] Men who do not meet enough girls of the right kind do not grow up with a good mental hygiene. If they do not learn at this age how to meet girls, and how to get along with them after meeting, they may find it hard to do so later. They then drift off into dormitories with their own kind and get into hopeless ruts. They may become desperate and try to escape from loneliness and a feeling of failure by cultivating the acquaintance of taxi dancers, "B girls," burlesque cuties and others whose "friendship" can be had on a cash rental basis. If they do not thus get trapped into unsatisfactory marriages, they may establish habits and attitudes which will make successful marriage unlikely.

Unless a man makes it a point consistently to go with girls of his own kind, girls whom he would not be afraid or ashamed to marry, it is far too easy to drift into attitudes of exploitation of the other sex. Many marriages have been damaged, or wrecked altogether, because one partner, or both, could not get rid of the habit of looking on the spouse as an object of exploitation. Such an attitude is at the opposite pole from the attitudes of sharing, of mutual trust, of reciprocal enlargement of personalities, which are involved in successful married life.

Where Do Men Meet the Girls They Marry?

How can young people form acquaintances that may lead to marriage?

Sometimes it is a mere accident; and there are enough of these romantic incidents to provide basis for fiction and the movies and to give unceasing and often ill-founded hope to many persons. Yvonne was one of a large party climbing Mount Shasta when she fell into a crevasse in the snow. She was rescued by three young men whom she had never seen before. One of them married her.

Luther was driver of an automobile full of people going on a picnic. There was an accident, and a girl in the car was badly hurt. He felt responsible and called on her frequently during her six months' convalescence, to inquire after her progress. He married her.

Alex was a piano salesman, who accompanied delivery of an instrument to a home. In the background there was a young woman who struck him as the shyest creature alive. When he went back a few weeks later to satisfy a complaint about the tone of the piano, this quiet and retiring young woman was again in the picture; he discovered that, being Italian, she talked mostly with her hands, and that those hands also played the piano particularly well. He became so fascinated watching her hands that he invented several other excuses to call at the home on presumed business, and eventually married her.

Eloise was visiting a CCC camp and wandered into the gymnasium where forty or fifty of the boys were participating, in one way or another, in a game of indoor baseball. A fellow who was generally regarded as the black sheep of the camp came up and tried to start a conversation. This alarmed one of the camp leaders; he felt that he ought to protect this stranger, so he led her out on some excuse. Marriage followed in due time.

Any reader can match such episodes from his own

knowledge. It is perhaps unfortunate that they do occur, for they feed the fires of Romantic Infantilism, at which so many people get their fingers burned: they lead men and women to drift along indefinitely, hoping that some miracle will happen for their benefit. Miracles do not happen often enough to keep up the vital statistics. The man who wants to meet girls will be more sensible if he first improves his own personality as much as possible, then studies feminine human nature, and finally follows the rules—the well-known, obvious rules of the game. First, he must go where girls are.

Where Are the Most Marriageable Women to Be Found?

There are probably plenty of girls in the man's own neighborhood, if he knows how to meet them, notwith-

State	Number of Marriageable Men	Number of Marriageable Men per 100 Marriageable Women
Nevada	2,133	158
Wyoming	4,002	142
Arizona	5,998	113
Montana	12,341	106
California	113,843	94
Washington	31,433	89
Idaho	7,774	87
Oregon	18,654	86
Michigan	87,202	86
New Mexico	5,670	83
South Dakota	16,384	83
Delaware	4,278	79
North Dakota	16,879	78

Wisconsin	66,367	77
Vermont	6,576	77
Colorado	17,665	75
Oklahoma	31,232	74
Texas	76,678	74
Maryland	27,932	73
District of Columbia	9,922	71
Illinois	146,667	69
Nebraska	26,917	68
Indiana	49,298	67
West Virginia	24,612	67
Iowa	46,530	67
New York	251,733	66
New Jersey	74,888	65
Kansas	30,749	65
Louisiana	24,110	65
Missouri	60,682	65
Ohio	109,635	65
Maine	12,278	64
Virginia	32,763	64
Florida	16,804	63
Kentucky	33,080	63
Pennsylvania	167,051	62
Arkansas	16,883	61
New Hampshire	7,774	59
Connecticut	30,138	59
Massachusetts	85,484	56
Utah	6,961	56
Georgia	28,040	56
Minnesota	51,877	56
Alabama	23,044	56
Mississippi	14,491	56
Tennessee	29,753	56
Rhode Island	12,757	54
North Carolina	32,632	52
South Carolina	14,117	52

standing that the distribution of marriageable men and marriageable women in the United States is uneven. Since the average man tends to marry a woman a few years younger than himself, it is not enough to take the census figures showing the number of men of twenty-five and the number of women of twenty-five and compare them. The men of twenty-five should be compared with the women of twenty-two, who, statistically speaking, are the ones they will marry.

To make the picture more definite, I have taken [84] all native-white, single women, twenty to twenty-nine, as representing, for the present purpose, the marriageable women of the United States. Most of the marriages each year are in this group. I have compared them with the group of "marriageable men" selected on the same basis (native-born whites) but of the age groups twenty-five to thirty-four. The accompanying table (from data of the United States Census of 1930) shows the distribution of marriageable women, in the special sense of these words that I have just defined, and the number of competitors a man will have to face in each state.

It is evident at a glance that there is a deficiency of men, or a surplus of women, in almost every state. A few western states have an excess of bachelors; and the same is true of a few industrial cities like Detroit, that support industries which hire predominantly young men. On the other hand, the agricultural states (where men marry early) and still more the states and cities that employ large numbers of young women, as, for example, in the textile mills of the south Atlantic coast, have large surpluses of spinsters. The men in these regions who have not married early have sometimes drifted away to other communities, where women had not taken all the jobs.

In general, therefore, young men seeking wives would find the largest range of choice in the eastern and southeastern states, while young women would do better in the western states. There are a few exceptions. Utah, for instance, has few marriageable men compared with the other Rocky Mountain states. This may be associated with the fact that the Mormon church sends out of the state a thousand or more of its picked young men each year on missions, but sends few women missionaries. Sometimes the young men make acquaintances in the mission field that end in marriage, and therefore do not return to lead their old neighbors to the altar. From the point of view of Utah girls, the church might do well to have all its young men marry before they leave home!

It is necessary, then, to go where girls are if you want to meet any. But it is equally necessary, in the second place, to find the right kind of girls, marriageable girls. You may be in a position to meet many girls who would be marriageable for some other fellow but not for you because they do not conform with your preferences in age, social background, education, race, religion—or for other reasons.

In the third place, it is not enough to be where girls are; you must be there under such circumstances that you can meet them and get acquainted with them informally and well. It is not enough, for instance, to go to the movies merely because there are a hundred girls in the audience—you have no way to get acquainted. "Pick-ups" in the educated part of the population account for only two or three marriages out of every hundred, and these few do not turn out as successfully as others.[108]

Social affairs in general too often provide only a formal or perfunctory kind of acquaintance. Albert and Alberta may meet through a series of such affairs; may go together for several years to the movies, to dances, and on automobile rides. They would say that they knew each other intimately; yet a moment's thought shows that neither has ever seen the other in the normal circumstances of life. They have always been in situations where each was putting his best foot forward, was deliberately trying to make a favorable impression. No wonder they find some surprises after marriage, when they live in a more normal, workaday atmosphere.

Advantages and Disadvantages of Social Life in Colleges.

The man who marries a co-ed with whom he has gone to school or college, has a great advantage. He has seen the Fair One under all sorts of conditions. He knows how she looks and acts at the Prom; he knows how she looks and acts at a seven o'clock class on the morning after the Prom. He has had a chance to study her disposition when she is working as well as when she is playing. Since such people are likely to have a good deal in common, as well, it is not surprising that such marriages turn out favorably. In one study,[28] only one such marriage in every seventy-five ended in the divorce court, as against one marriage in every five or six for the United States as a whole.

Colleges and high schools [78] are now making a much greater effort to provide their students with a normal social life. Probably too much stress is laid on dancing, since this does not give people the best opportunity to know each other. Dances might well be supplemented more liberally with picnics, hikes, beach parties; still more with working committees and other groups in which boys and girls could learn to co-operate with each other, at the same time getting the greater acquaintance which is possible through work.

Social life in many of the larger co-educational colleges and universities is seriously hindered by the "rating and dating complex" which restricts the range of social acquaintance for almost every one.[123] Members of certain organizations or cliques will lose prestige if they date with any except members of certain other organizations or cliques. By this false set of values, they themselves are the greatest losers; and there are already indications that the reign of this kind of organized snobbishness in the colleges is tottering.

Parenthetically, it is interesting to note the present popularity of "blind dating" throughout the United States. It is a great step forward, even if only a first step, toward getting away from an over-restricted social life. Of course you will draw a blank occasionally; but that is the way you learn the game.

If one wants to know where to make acquaintances that might lead to marriage, the scientific way to proceed is to ask those who have husbands and wives to tell where they found them. Such a study is easily made; and the accompanying table presents the facts of 9,081 marriages, collected by my students in many parts of the United States during the past twelve years. From a study of this table it is evident that, for educated people, the educational system itself is now the principal matrimonial agency. More partners meet by going to school together than in any other one way. Introduction by friends in the ordinary course of social life is second in importance; third place is occupied by meetings in the course of business. Perhaps the two persons worked in the same place; perhaps one was a customer. Imogene had her tonsils removed by a young surgeon, who fell in love with her. Theodore was clerking in a grocery store and became interested in a young woman who dropped in every day to do the marketing for the family. For many people who are in great cities, without any influential circle of friends and relatives to help them, and who during their school years did not make acquaintances leading to marriage, business associations are the chief, sometimes almost the only, source of meetings. The other items in the list are self-explanatory. It should be remembered that this represents the meetings of people in what I have called the educated part of the population. In the stratum of skilled and semi-skilled labor, conditions may be different. It appears that meetings in places of commercial entertainment, such as dance halls and skating rinks, play a much more important part for them than for the educated group.[98]

Place of First Meeting of Educated Married Couples

PLACE	NUMBER	PER CENT
Educational system	2297	25.3
Homes of friends	1656	18.2
Business contacts	1143	12.9
Church and church social organizations	927	10.2
Propinquity	867	9.5
Private recreation	747	8.2
Travel, vacation, resort	638	7.0
Commercial recreation	345	3.7
Miscellaneous	251	2.7
Pick-ups	210	2.3
	9081	100.0

It would be desirable to know more definitely whether there is any great advantage of one place of meeting over another in the future happiness of the marriage. Data are available [108] for only 745 marriages, much too small a number to answer such an important question. These data do not reveal any marked differences.

How Can Happiness in Marriage Be Measured?

To determine the happiness of any particular group of marriages, one needs to know the happiness of all marriages. This involves problems which have received attention from many students. The first problem, of course, is to decide how happiness can be measured. It is at once evident that there is no objective yardstick. Happiness is merely a state of mind. If you think you are happy, and if those who know you best also think you are happy, then you are happy; one can hardly go farther than that. Attempts of various investigators to measure the happiness of marriage have therefore tended to reduce themselves to some such findings. Refinement is added by having husbands and wives check things which they do not like in their spouses (husbands despise a nagging and slovenly wife; wives hate a selfish and dishonest husband); by having them list the number of disagreements and express an opinion on the seriousness of these disagreements; by counting the number of their joint activities, and by estimating their general state of mental hygiene. In such ways, several predictive scales of fairly satisfactory character have been produced. The fact that most of these give fairly concordant results is reassuring.[109]

It is at once evident that most of the marriages in the educated part of the population are happy. So much is said of divorce and maladjustment that this prime fact should be borne in mind. It would be even more correct to say that most of the people who marry are happy, for the divorce rate is increased by repeaters. One man who is married and divorced four times will offset, in the statistics, four men whose first and only marriage is completely happy.

During the past fifteen years I have had occasion to tabulate, for different purposes, nearly 20,000 marriages in different parts of the country. The happiness was rated by those who knew them intimately. A number of samples are given in the appendices. These studies show consistently that from 60 to 75 per cent of marriages of more than five years duration, in the educated part of the population, are regarded by those who knew them well as definitely happy.

How does the happiness of the marriage correlate with the duration of the marriage? Do people start out at a high level and then slump gradually to a stale and profitless routine in later years? Or does each additional year of marriage tend to add to the happiness of the partners? A study of 2,138 marriages (see Appendix II) indicates that neither of these suppositions is true. In the course of a lifetime some marriages are deteriorating, and even go to pieces in divorce; others are improving. The percentage of definitely happy marriages after twenty years is about the same that it was after two years.

The Majority of All Marriages Are Happy.

In some ways, a rating of happiness by close friends and relatives may be more trustworthy than the statements of the partners themselves. I believe that close friends and relatives are not often deceived in such a matter, and that their ratings are worthy of confidence. The same method was adopted by Richard O. Lang when a graduate student at the University of Chicago; he got students in various colleges to report on the happiness of 8,263 marriages.[40] The grouping was a little different from mine, but the marriages should be fairly comparable; it is therefore interesting to see how Dr. Lang's cases were distributed:

Very happy	39.5 per cent
Happy	25.4 " "
Average	19.2 " "
Unhappy	10.0 " "
Very unhappy	5.8 " "

From any point of view, a substantial majority of these marriages is evidently considered, by the intimates of the family, to be definitely happy.

If people are asked to rate their own marriages, they are often a little more favorable to themselves than are outsiders.* Perhaps they say to themselves, "I suppose I'm not entirely happy; but then, who is? If I had it to do over again, I should doubtless marry the same girl. On the whole, I guess I'm entitled to consider myself happy by any ordinary standard."

In a study [17] of 1,000 educated married women, 87 per cent definitely declared themselves to be happy without any qualifications. In a study [11] of 526 couples in Illinois, 63 per cent declared themselves to be either happy or very happy, while 14 per cent thought their happiness "only average." In a study [108] of 792 couples in California who rated their own marriages, 82 per cent of the men and 85 per cent of the women felt that their happiness was "above the average." The groups com-

* The difference is not great statistically, however. In a study [11] on this particular point, it was found that self-ratings and ratings by friends correlated to the extent of .91.

pared in these studies were fairly representative of what one might call the average normal part of the educated American population. One can properly draw the conclusion from these studies and others that a large majority of such persons find happiness in marriage.

The search for a partner, then, is hopeful. It is not necessary to discover some superwoman for your purpose—unless you are a superman. If all these people found happiness in marriage, there is no reason why you should not do the same.

CHAPTER IV

AND WHAT WILL *SHE* THINK OF *YOU*?

THE average young woman expects, or at least hopes, to find three qualities in the man she marries:

1. Strength.

From the beginning of time, woman has had to entrust her fate to the man she married. Child-bearing handicapped her for protecting herself from enemies, or for ranging far afield to gather food. Not merely her comfort, but her life, might depend on getting a husband who was able to take good care of her.

In later times this need of protection, this requirement of strength and power in the man to whom she entrusted herself, has naturally been somewhat modified in expression. Financial strength may now be more desirable than physical strength. A "good provider" may be more useful to her than an overgrown bully ready to beat up any other male who looks sidewise at her in the street. But the man who wants to get a desirable wife will have to offer some sort of strength, unless he is satisfied to use weakness as his stock in trade and attract the pity of some motherly female who will marry him merely to take care of him. Successful marriages of this

48

kind do exist, but they always run the risk of difficulties later. The man may grow up emotionally and come to think that his position is humiliating. His attitude will then change, so that his wife will feel that he is no longer grateful to her for the mothering that she has been lavishing on him. She thereupon loses the only satisfaction that she could expect to get—the emotional satisfaction that one might get from the gratitude of a child that looked up to mama as the source of all good. Thenceforth there might be little of value to either one of them in that marriage.

What kind of strength are you going to offer? Not all men can be prizefighters, not all can be millionaires. Not all have high social position, which is one of the things a girl is likely to seek, since the woman's social rank in American society is usually dependent upon that of her husband, not vice versa, and since the happiness of the marriage is influenced more by the man's family background than by that of the wife.[11]

If you bear in mind the biological background of this feminine attraction to strength and power—if you recall that it stands primarily for dependability and protection—then you will see that almost any man can meet the requirements if he wants to. He cannot become a 200-pound athlete at will, he cannot become a bank president at will; but he *can* attain financial honesty and dependability, emotional maturity and moral worth. These, being much more durable, offer a wife much better protection than do some other kinds of wealth and strength. Intelligent girls know this. Foolish ones may be carried away by more flashy or beefy attributes; but you would not waste your time on the foolish virgins, anyhow.

Traditional masculine manifestations of strength are aggressiveness, assumption of the initiative in dealing with women, physical courage, moral courage, and willingness to assume responsibility. The man who wants women to respect and admire him can cultivate these attributes; but there are dangers. He may be merely bossy and domineering; or he may be so vain, conceited, and egotistical that he is ridiculous when not actually offensive. Few men succeed in avoiding these difficulties altogether; for egotism is one of the besetting sins of the male, as "cattiness" is of the female. Let me give a few illustrations of the infantile male who loves himself so much that there is very little room left in his world for anyone else, except as a worshiper:

He ignores most people because, he says, they are so inferior that they bore him.

He does not desire seriously and vigorously to overcome his weaknesses.

Entering a room with a group, he at once picks out the best chair and settles down in it.

When he meets opposition to his plans, he becomes angry and tries to force agreement regardless of the circumstances.

He is very eager to receive praise before others, and always feels that he is entitled to it.

He will not play unless he can be "it."

When his partner makes a mistake, he acts as if it were a personal affront and reprimands her publicly.

When someone makes a witty remark, he laughs louder than the rest and at once tries to improve on it in order to get the spotlight.

He tries to monopolize the conversation in a group and obviously enjoys it greatly.

He tends to disregard social conventions except when the penalties are too great, or when the penalty will fall on himself more than on his partner.

When introduced to a person who is apparently his superior, he seems to look upon him as a disagreeable competitor and to do everything he can to show that "I, too, am an important personage."

He thinks he is irresistible with women.

Anyone can continue the list indefinitely from his own observation. Such behavior is often believed, by the man himself, to be a display of strength; it is in fact merely self-assertion based on infantile conceit.

The roots of normal masculine self-esteem go far back; and there are plenty of examples from other animals, the peacock being a familiar illustration. But women often have good reason to complain—and do complain, loudly and long—of the childish vanity, the unwarranted conceit, the easily hurt feelings of men with whom they associate. Build your strength on something more substantial than conceit, if you expect it to sustain a wife.

2. *Comradeship.*

There may be parts of society in which the woman admires "caveman" tactics and does not feel sure of a man's affection unless he beats her occasionally. It is safe to say that no one who belongs to such a stratum of society will ever read this book, and that men of the class likely to see this chapter will make a better impression on women by treating them as equals than by treating them as inferiors.

Questioning of 250 well educated and very happily married women revealed that they admired their husbands particularly because the latter offered comradeship.[129] These men did not act as if they were afraid of their wives, or as if their wives were children to whom they had to "talk down"—children who could not be trusted to understand the family's financial affairs or take an intelligent part in a conversation based on the news of the day. The girls who will make the best wives are, in most instances, those who will most desire intellectual companionship and insist on it (see also Chapter X).

This does not mean merely that a man must be congenial and affable in general terms. It means that he must study a girl's nature; learn the things that appeal to her; treat her feminine peculiarities with interested respect, rather than amused tolerance or contempt; and maintain a sense of humor *with* her, not at her expense.

A group of psychologists at the University of Minnesota published [18] a study of conversation, made by the

simple process of listening in on talk in public places—
in a word, eavesdropping. Many men have done this,
but they did not call it psychology and get college credit
for it. They therefore missed three conclusions which
this group drew from their experiences:

(a) When men are talking with men, they talk about
things that interest men.

(b) When women are talking with women, they
talk about things that interest women.

(c) When men and women are talking together, they
talk a good deal about things that do not interest either
one of them!

Life is too short for this! Any bright girl would
probably assert that it is easy to carry on a conversation
with a man which will at least interest *him*: all she has
to do is to lean back comfortably, look into his eyes and
say, "Now tell me some more about yourself." Men
might similarly make some effort to understand the interests of women; and, especially after marriage, take a
little more interest in their wives' clothes, home-making,
and social concerns. Many women complain that the
young man of today wants to be merely a passenger; he
will make no real effort to be a good host, or even to
meet the obligations of a guest.[88] The man who wants
to be regarded by any woman as a real comrade should
give some thought to this indictment.

3. *Romance.*

I will deal with romance more fully in Chapter IX. At this point it is necessary only to insist that in addition to strength and comradeship, every woman expects that the man of her choice will satisfy her need of a love-life; and unless he is able to do this he is not likely to be the man of her choice for any length of time.

Sometimes a woman's aspirations in this direction are adolescent, perhaps neurotic; but even when they are reasonable, she is too often disappointed. Young men who are otherwise superior may fail egregiously as lovers.

Able, ambitious, and hard-working young men often have too many other interests and have their hands too full to be able to spend much of their time in feminine society. As a consequence, they are novices when it comes to making love; and competitors of much less real worth, who have devoted more attention to studying women, gain desirable wives to whom they are not entitled.

This is a serious situation in every way; and it is complicated by the fact that, while some girls are dangerously easy to marry, the most desirable ones are correspondingly hard to win. Sometimes a superior man, feeling conscious of his superiority, believes that he has nothing to do but to offer himself to the finest girl of his acquaintance, and that she will jump at the opportunity to acquire such a good husband. He soon learns that superior girls do not respond in that way; and unless he studies his failures and applies his knowledge to good purpose, he is likely to end by marrying the traditional landlady's daughter or some other girl who will not wait to be asked twice.

Probably it would be safe to say that the more desirable a girl is, the more difficult she is to win. In the first place, she knows her own value and does not propose to cheapen herself by giving herself away too easily; in the second place, she demands more in a mate; in the third place, competition is keener.

Instead of letting some loafer get away with a better wife than he deserves, the intelligent young man will therefore devote as much time and thought to preparation for marriage as he will to preparation for his profession; and an important part of this preparation will be to try to find out how to please her. This will require somewhat more attention to grooming, to etiquette, to social convention and so-called cultural interests, than a good many young men are accustomed to give.[98] There is a widespread complaint among college girls, for instance, that many otherwise superior young men not only lack polish, but even lack cleanliness; that they are so much wrapped up in themselves that it is almost impossible for them to understand that they owe something to the young woman who spends all her allowance on clothing and beauty shops in order to impress them favorably.

Woman wants a man who embodies power; and of course she gets a great feeling of superiority from the reflection that *she* can dominate this powerful creature who dominates everyone else. A recognition of this feeling will prevent one from taking some manifestations of it too seriously.

Cultivation of these admired characteristics—strength, comradeship, and what may for the present purpose be called tenderness—will help any man to pass his examinations in dealing with the other sex. Many girls, even though college graduates, have been so badly educated as to the difference between the sexes that they do not know what to expect of men, and expect something they are not likely to find in ordinary masculine behavior. This makes the examinations more difficult.

For a generation or more, until the past few years, it has been the custom for many women educators in high schools and colleges to minify the differences in the behavior of the sexes. Girls who came under the influence of these feminists were told that the alleged differences between the sexes were merely superstitions, fostered by men who wanted to make woman feel inferior. "Don't pay any attention to them: we're all human beings, and we'll get along perfectly well if we just remember that we're all human beings."

With such a start, the girl married and supposed she was marrying a human being. Pretty soon she found that her husband was not acting like a human being—at least, not if she knew what a human being was like. Then she was in trouble.[129] Why was her husband acting this way? It must be because he was mad at her, or was no longer interested in her, or was interested in someone else, or was trying to punish her for something she did not know she had done—anything except the plain fact that he was a mere male, and that mere males normally behave that way!

Until women get a better education in this respect, men will continue from time to time to be misunderstood, as they usually believe they are anyway. Apart from the great masculine self-esteem, which is sometimes hard for women to accept, there are two peculiarities of the masculine make-up that particularly cause misunderstandings. One is the greater ease or readiness of sexual stimulation of the male (see Chapter V); the other, what has been called "gang sociality." This is the tendency of a man to want to be with his own sex once in a while; to want to get away from female dominance or even association. Probably it goes back to primitive times and springs from an unconscious fear of the female, which is pretty widely spread among men. At any rate, man has been domesticated rather recently; the process is not yet complete; and he does not want it to be too complete. It is necessary to his comfort and self-esteem that he get off occasionally with his own kind, far from the madding girls, where he and his fellows can slap each other on the back, assure each other that they are free and untrammeled he-men; and then go back to their domestication eagerly!

Given a choice, the average woman would usually prefer a social affair where men are present, to a "hen party." It is hard for her to understand that men like to get away from female society occasionally; that such a tendency is no reflection on her; and that she will have a better partner if she does not hold him with too tight a rein!

A group of one hundred women, asked by me to name the peculiarities of women which were most frequently misunderstood or disregarded by men, to the disadvantage of those men in their relationships with women, selected the following:

(a) Slower sexual excitability.

(b) Fluctuation of mood; tendency to be depressed or irritable at certain parts of the menstrual cycle, for instance.[16]

(c) Importance attached to small attentions: remembering dates of anniversaries, sending little gifts and notes, and the like.

(d) Importance attached to matters of social status and social repute, fulfillment of social obligations.

(e) Desire for recognition of equality, eagerness for genuine comradeship, resentment of condescension.

Of course there are all kinds of women in the world, but the man who wants educated American women to think well of him will make no mistake if he considers those five points carefully.

*Normal Masculinity Must
Be Cultivated.*

Women do not admire a man who is a sissy. I asked another one hundred educated women to state whether they preferred, as friends and husbands, men who were highly masculine, average, or low in masculinity. Only three expressed a preference for the latter.

"I prefer a man who has a *slight* tendency to be effeminate," one wrote. "I have found this type of man to be more understanding and sympathetic and a much more intelligent comrade than the extreme masculine type. The more effeminate man is more responsive to beauty in music, art, and literature and is emotionally moved by such things. The more masculine type is too responsive to sex."

"I just can't live with the 'dominant male' type who is a natural bully in his role of male," wrote another, who declared that she liked "a man with the virtues generally attributed to women." A third agreed substantially.

Of the remaining ninety-seven women, thirty-three preferred a man who was highly masculine, sixty-four voted for one who was just average. The general argument of the latter was that the ultra-masculine type tended to be boorish, aggressively self-conscious, given to "cave man" tactics, and lacking in appreciation of the things that interest women.

One might debate the question whether a highly masculine type need have these defects; if so, women would be justified in objecting. The concepts of masculinity and femininity are vague and traditional, but it was clear that the women who admired masculinity had in mind strength, good sportsmanship, efficiency—the sort of traits on which a woman can depend for protection and progress; in short, very much the traits that I outlined earlier in this chapter.

How far is the women's preference for men of only average masculinity justified? I have no figures to show whether such men make a wife happier, but I have some data which indicate that these men themselves are happier in marriage (see Appendix III). Men and women students furnished particulars concerning 1,493 men intimately known to them, rating these men as to masculinity and also as to their marital happiness. They classified 36 per cent as highly masculine, 44 per cent as average, and 20 per cent as low.

Of the highly masculine, 67 per cent were considered to be happy in marriage; of the intermediates, 72 per cent; of the low in masculinity, only 54 per cent.

This is no more than most people would expect; and it is important to recognize that even of those on the effeminate side, an actual majority were happily married. Presumably they had found the kind of wives they wanted. Nevertheless, the well-differentiated male has the advantage; and, since this is something that, within limits, can be cultivated, the man who wants women to think well of him should cultivate a normal masculinity of appearance and behavior. For this purpose, it is unfortunate that boys' education nowadays is so largely dominated by women, and with so few men in their lives. This—or something else—is producing undesirable results. Indeed, one investigator, after measuring the masculinity of men in all sorts of professions, concluded that the only he-men left in the country were engineers and farmers, and that even these are in danger!

The preference of women for definitely masculine men and the greater happiness of these men in marriage justify increased attention to the development of more of the traditional masculine characteristics in American boys. This does not call for the encouragement of obsolete patriarchal patterns, nor of dueling and cock-fighting; but of those fundamental patterns of strength, dependability, and initiative, which are not merely compatible with comradeship but invaluable in building up a worth-while comradeship with women. You may not be handsome, you may not be rich, you may not be a genius; but these are not the qualities most needed in marriage. The qualities that are essential, and that are consciously sought by young women, are qualities that you can cultivate for yourself.

CHAPTER V

REMEMBER, YOU DO *NOT* UNDERSTAND WOMEN

THE average man, it has been said, can tell all he knows in two hours. After that he begins to talk about women.

It is too much to expect that any man will understand women, since women do not even understand themselves. But a great deal of misunderstanding would be avoided if men would merely understand that they do *not* understand women. Then they would proceed more cautiously!

Most of the trouble is due to the fact that boys expect girls to behave as they themselves would; and vice versa. It would be safer to assume that, in any situation, each sex will behave differently from the other. They act differently, think differently, talk differently—at least, they do not use the same words to mean the same thing. To take the stock illustration: if a man declares, "I haven't anything to wear," it doesn't mean at all what it would if his wife said it.

If one wanted to find a formula to illustrate the profound mental differences between the two sexes, he might take that pair of commonplace remarks: "Business is business" and "I haven't anything to wear." "Business is business" is an axiom which symbolizes the soul of the male. No woman—in orthodox masculine opinion—ever understands the meaning of it completely, although she understands perfectly well that it covers a multitude of sins. But no man expects a woman to grasp the full and profound import of it, any more than he expects her to be able to read a railroad time-table correctly or to play a good game of poker. It is out of her sphere.

On the other hand, no experienced woman expects her husband to know what she is talking about when he invites her to go somewhere and she responds, "But, dear, I haven't anything to wear." Perhaps he has heard this so often that it provokes him to a mighty and righteous wrath. "Oh, you haven't anything to wear, haven't you?" he demands with incandescent sarcasm, as he grabs her by the hand, drags her across the room, and throws open the closet door. "You haven't anything to wear. Well, what are all these?" and he points to a closet full of attractive dresses, hanger after hanger neatly aligned.

It is simply useless for her to try to answer his question. He would not know what she is talking about.

She could easily take each dress in turn and explain it to him:

This one—she has begun to think that the waist line is a little bit too low.

This one—she never could get the hem to hang evenly all around.

This one—is just a rag.

This one—she wore to the same place last year.

This one—she has no hat to match.

This one—she has no handbag to match.

This one—she has no slippers to match.

This one—the slippers that match it are too tight for her in warm weather.

This one—would be just the thing if she could wear her winter coat with it, but it is now so late in the season that she would have to wear her summer coat, and the dress would hang down at least an inch below it.

This one—she used to like pretty well, but she has had it so long that she hates the sight of it.

This one—she never did like very well.

And so on, to the back of the closet. But it is no use; he would not understand!

The proprietor of a nudist camp told me that most of his clients were not young people, but middle-aged married couples. Perhaps that tendency will continue. A trip to the nudist colony is the only entertainment to which a man can invite his wife with the certainty that she will not reply, "But, dear, I haven't anything to wear."

Women Have Had Little Training in Team-work.

While I do not pretend to understand women, it seems to me one might get some possible clues by considering the differences in the history of the two sexes during the last million years or so. Man has been largely the hunter and fighter. Both of these occupations have required team-work, co-operation, and discipline. If the men of a tribe could not work together successfully in such ways, they were exterminated, and the progress of mankind was continued by some group with greater co-operative ability. Man is weak enough in these respects, at the present time; but it would be surprising if he had not in this way developed a certain amount of sex solidarity and teamwork and a code of sportsmanship, so-called. But this was certainly not paralleled very closely in the development of woman.

Woman's work during these long ages was much more individual. Why should anyone expect her to have developed an equal degree of solidarity with her own sex, and a code of sportsmanship and good fellowship identical with that of the male? Biologists would hold it almost inconceivable that she should have done so. She would naturally develop along the lines indicated by her own work. There is no reason whatever to expect women to have the same code of fair play and sportsmanship that men have developed through 100,000 years of hunting and fighting expeditions. Women did not need it. There is no reason whatever to measure women by a masculine yardstick or to measure men by a feminine yardstick.

Not only was woman's work more likely to be individual, but an important part of it was concerned with getting and holding a man. If she did not succeed in this, her peculiarities would disappear from the race because she would leave no offspring. And since nothing succeeds like success, she was justified in doing anything to achieve this end—to get not merely a husband, but a good husband; one who would stand by her and their children. In this undertaking she had to compete with other women as well as deal with the male; and in her competition with the male she was handicapped by his greater physical strength and aggressiveness. She had to overcome his strength with her weakness somehow and at the same time circumvent her rivals among the other women.

Since success in this attempt was literally a matter of life and death, and since those women who succeeded best would be those who had the best chance of perpetuating their patterns through posterity, one would expect women to develop characteristic and effective methods of meeting this problem, different from those of the male. I think no open-minded person can doubt that they have done so.

No one should be surprised, therefore, if women do not behave as men do, particularly when they are dealing with men. No one should be surprised if they are fickle, deceitful, intriguing, or anything else, if that has been found useful for their purposes. I am not praising or blaming any such behavior, if it exists; I am merely pointing out why it might have come into existence, and trying to emphasize the folly of judging it by purely masculine standards.

Woman Has a Right to Change Her Mind.

It was, I repeat, necessary for a woman not merely to get a husband, but to get the best husband possible. She risked a good deal more in the mating than he did, since it would probably be followed by her pregnancy, certainly not by his. It was plain common sense, therefore, that she should be (1) slow to accept a male who offered himself [58] and (2) ready to change her mind, even after acceptance, if she could better her prospects.

1. *Among most of the higher animals* the female is supposed (and there is some evidence to confirm the supposition) to exercise deliberate choice as to the male with whom she mates. This is certainly true of mankind. To make any choice possible, it is necessary that the female be not too prompt in choosing. If she were ready, as is the ordinary male, to mate with the first individual of the other sex who appeared, there would be an end of sexual selection. A certain amount of "sex antagonism", a slowness to be aroused, and the requirement of a long period of courtship on the part of the male, give her a chance to look out for her own interests. During this process some other and more attractive male may appear; or the female may reject the first applicant altogether and withdraw from the scene. This primitive biological pattern is as evident in modern society as in the jungle.

2. *Suppose she has agreed to accept some male,* and a better one comes along. She would be a fool if she

failed to drop Number One and take Number Two. This fact has been recognized widely enough, subject to many forms of social control. If a mating has been actually consummated, it has usually been expected that the partners would stand by their choice. They have then accepted all sorts of responsibilities—biological, psychological, social, economic—which they cannot repudiate. But if they have merely talked about it, the girl is not necessarily bound.

Society recognizes an interesting standard of double morality in this connection, associated with the fact that marriage is primarily for the protection of the woman and the children. If a man has proposed to a girl and she has accepted him, he is supposed to stand by his word. To let him break it would be to put a premium on irresponsibility—the one defect above all others which women have to fear, and which society has to fear. It has taken millions of years to get the male to accept and live up to his responsibility in the partnership, and he cannot be allowed to play fast and loose with it now. The man who jilts his fiancée is therefore not admired as clever, not even by other men; he is reprobated, and in some communities may even be sued for breach of promise and punished severely.

On the other hand, the woman who breaks off an engagement is not an outcast; she may have been engaged to half a dozen men and merely be looked upon as rather smart. The man who tried to bring suit against her for breach of promise would be laughed out of court.

Of course these breach-of-promise suits have become more and more notorious as blackmailing enterprises, until many states have wisely made them illegal. Nevertheless, the fact that they exist, or have recently existed, proves that public opinion dimly saw some of the biological factors involved: the greater significance of marriage, biologically, to woman than to man; the fact that the initiative was largely in his hands, so that she had to work indirectly; and the importance to her of getting the best possible husband and of not being deprived of a favorable opportunity on a technicality, so to speak. A good marriage is too important to her to be trifled with, and public opinion has been willing to protect her in any way that it could because of her greater stake in the proceedings. This greater stake, and the general recognition of it, could not help influencing her entire behavior: her attitude toward men, toward courtship, and toward marriage.

Any man who thinks over these differences in the historical position of the two sexes can easily develop the subject further for himself. He cannot help seeing that the difference in the attitude of the two sexes toward mating; the relative lack of team-work and discipline in women's work; the economic dependence of the female on the male, at least during the period when she was most handicapped by child-bearing; the need of holding her own with her mate in spite of his greater physical strength and aggressiveness—all these and similar conditions would bring about habits of thought and methods of action among women that would often differ from those of the male. By a study along these lines, one might get some idea of what women are like and how they are likely to behave.

The Inferiority Complexes
of Educated Women.

So far as educated women in America are concerned, however, the study is complicated by the fact that many of them have developed an inferiority complex based on their femaleness, and that their traditional patterns are distorted by their attempt to repudiate these patterns —without, of course, being able to repudiate the biological differences that underlie them.

Too many girls are brought up to think that being born a female is a misfortune. As far back as they can remember, they have been prevented from doing interesting things because of this handicap. "Little girls don't do such things." "That's all right for boys, but you mustn't do it." They grow up feeling that the world is against them; that it is a man's world; and that they are cut off from many satisfactions that should be theirs, just because they are females.

Men sometimes have reason to take the opposite view: to think that this is a woman's world in which men never get a square deal. It is an interesting sidelight on the unsound biological basis of a good deal of modern education, and a commentary on the unwisdom of mothers and other relatives who force a girl to grow up sympathizing with herself for being a girl. Yet no one can doubt that this is the fact: questionnaires have shown that a majority of educated women have at times wished they had been born boys. Not many normal men ever wished that they had been born girls.

A girl's whole future may be colored by this "masculine protest." She may avoid marriage. If she marries, she may be a frigid wife. Or she may react even more aggressively to the way in which she feels the world is wronging her sex, and become a feminist.

For the present purpose, feminists may be described as women who have inferiority complexes based on the fact of their sex; and who compensate for these by attempting on the one hand to depreciate the male, on the other hand to assume as many as possible of the traditional male habits, attitudes, and prerogatives. It is not surprising that this paradoxical behavior puzzles men.

When a young man, therefore, is trying to understand some girl and treat her intelligently on the assumption that she is a woman, he may be baffled by the fact that she is unconsciously trying *not* to be a woman; that she resents it if he treats her as a woman; and equally resents it if he does not!

What are you going to do with a girl like that?

The first thing to do is to identify her.

Probably the most characteristic symptom of this frame of mind is aggressiveness on the part of the woman. You will not have to look far for it.

A generation or two ago the man who was about to be married made all the arrangements with the minister, who might not see the bride until the day of the wedding. Recalling this, an elderly clergyman remarked to me recently that the arrangement had been reversed. Now it is the woman who calls on him to make arrangements for the wedding, and he may not see the groom until the time for the ceremony arrives.*

This observation symbolizes the change that has taken place in the relation of the sexes during recent years. Women have, in their dealings with men, become more and more the possessors of the initiative. The male is more and more led, guided, managed, bossed, directed, and controlled by the female.

In other mammals the reverse is still the case: the male is the aggressive sex. Since this has been the case for millions of years, it is to be expected that the attempt to override this deep-seated tendency will mean discomfort, dissatisfaction, and unhappiness for both sexes.

A man can keep away from the more grotesque consequences, from the two-fisted he-woman who thinks she will be admired by all the boys because she goes after them on their own ground as a hail-fellow-well-met. Behind her back she is either laughed at, or despised, or a little of each. But what are you going to do with the subtler and more pervasive manifestations of the "masculine protest"?

It is no use to be satisfied with condemning the mother and teachers who brought her up that way. The

---

* In which case he is not living up to his own responsibilities. Nowadays progressive and socially minded clergymen insist on seeing both parties to a marriage some days before the wedding, so that they may find out whether these persons are really prepared to marry and may give them any additional help necessary to make the marriage turn out well.

safest course to follow is to study and respect her personality rather than merely her sexuality. No woman wants to be admired *merely* because she is a female. If she has merely femaleness, she has nothing more than is possessed by one half the entire human species. This is no credit to her. She ought to be resentful if she finds she is valued for nothing except femaleness.

When any woman is willing to make that her main appeal, it is good evidence that her mental hygiene is impaired. The prostitute trades on her femaleness and often tries to protect herself from the resulting mental conflict by splitting her personality. Her femaleness she regards more or less unconsciously as something apart from the rest of her personality. She will give a man the use of that (remaining frigid and merely pretending interest); but he need not think that he is getting the rest of her personality with it—she will keep that for herself, or for some other man.

The psychology of the sexually aggressive girl who is occasionally found in high school, college, or afterward, is somewhat different (at least, ordinarily) and equally abnormal. The prostitute, as a commercial convenience, splits her personality and offers men the use of her femaleness only, while at the same time secretly despising them and taking pleasure in the feeling that she is making fools of them. The over-aggressive girl to whom I am referring is seeking primarily to get attention, to feel important, to overcome a sense of inadequacy and a fear of not being wanted. She is therefore exploiting her femaleness as the only bait she has, the only attraction she possesses, and is hoping, not to keep her personality separated from her femaleness as does the prostitute, but to have her personality tied to her femaleness so that the man who does not desire her personality will nevertheless have to take it in order to get the femaleness which she supposes to be so attractive to him. It is scarcely necessary to add that she is often disappointed!

Each of these types is recognized easily enough as abnormal and not admirable. The girl who wants to repudiate her femaleness altogether is equally abnormal and unadmirable, but fortunately rare. Most of the remainder, and certainly all those worth marrying, may be put in one large group which wants to keep its femaleness and the remaining and much larger part of its personality inseparable and indivisible. If attention is paid to the personality as a whole, the femaleness will be included in it, where it belongs.

In other words, I believe the intelligent and superior girl who has a "masculine protest" (you will be surprised to find how numerous these girls are) is prepared, at least consciously, to recognize that femaleness is a part of her personality; but she will not tolerate being treated condescendingly, as if she were "nothing but a female"—and I am now, of course, using the word to refer not merely to sexuality but to everything that can be included under the heading of femaleness. The men to whom she objects (and you will be surprised to find how numerous *they* are) are those who act as if she were some sort of an inferior creature; or as if her personality, her intelligence, her ambitions, her achievements, were all quite secondary and subordinate to her femaleness.

Woman's Lack of Accepted Patterns.

If these varying currents and tides in a woman's nature cause some confusion to the men associated with her, it must not be supposed that they do not cause confusion to her as well, even though she does not analyze the nature of it. The average educated girl is the victim of a confusion of tongues, because she has no simple and universally accepted pattern to follow, as her forebears had a century ago. Her great-grandmother had a simple pattern before her; everyone knew what it was; all she had to do was to follow that pattern successfully and she would be universally admired. That pattern, of course, involved marriage, motherhood, and the efficient management of the important industrial enterprise that was the home.

Her great-granddaughter has no sort of pattern that is universally accepted. On the one hand, she has a natural tendency toward marriage and parenthood; on the other hand, she is continually being urged, implicitly or explicitly, toward a "career"; and she cannot help observing that those women who get the most public attention in the world are not the wives and mothers, but the childless careerists. Most of her teachers are in this group and may unconsciously influence her.

She can never quite make up her mind what she ought to do: whether she should marry or forego marriage for a career; whether she should try to have a marriage and a career at the same time; whether, if she marries, she should have children; whether, if she has children, she should take care of them at home or hire someone else to do that while she works outside. All these possibilities are continually before her; and when she has adopted one, she cannot help wondering whether she should not have chosen some other. Frequently, though quite unconsciously, she oscillates between them; and her husband, poor fellow, trails along trying to outguess her and usually about twenty-four hours behind her in the guessing game. No wonder she complains that he does not understand her!

If women should ever make up their minds how they want to be treated, they will have no difficulty in getting men to treat them that way. Meanwhile, men will have to study their partners, try to respect their wishes, and still be prepared for surprises.

I have not mentioned some of the well-known causes of difficulty, such as woman's monthly rhythm,[16] which often leads the unsuspecting male to misinterpret her mood. And of course I have not tried to tell anybody how to understand women! No two are alike, anyway; but on the average they certainly do behave somewhat differently from men. If you devote your life to trying to find out *how*, you will never lack for entertainment and instruction.

CHAPTER VI

WHAT WILL YOUR PARENTS SAY?

DESPITE the theory that young people choose their own partners in the United States, parents still have a good deal to say. If they do not select a son-in-law or daughter-in-law for themselves, as in some other countries, they sometimes claim and occasionally exercise the power of veto. Girls encounter more obstacles in this direction than do boys;[15] but you yourself may find, whether you be eighteen, twenty-eight, or thirty-eight, that your parents hope, or even expect, to influence your choice of a wife.

This is partly force of habit. For years they guided your decisions. They encouraged certain friendships and discouraged others. They helped you to select a college or a job. Perhaps they got the job for you. That was only a year or two ago. Now you are facing a new decision, much more important to you and to them than any you have ever made. Of course they cannot help being interested.

How far should you consider their wishes, or even consult them?

That depends on the reason for their concern; and it may be hard for you, as their son, to evaluate this. On the one hand, they are more experienced; they have seen a lot of mistakes, perhaps even made a few themselves. They are not so easily moonstruck as you are, and they feel that they would be criminally guilty if they sat idly by and saw you shipwreck yourself, without trying to save you.

On the other hand, they may be deeply involved emotionally. They may simply have a mania for bossing other people. They may be the kind that is always trying to run somebody else's affairs. They may belong to the rule-or-ruin party.

How can you decide?

Observation shows that this is one of the most difficult problems for young people to meet. Many of them have not yet wholly emancipated themselves from their own homes. They may still be in leading strings. On the other hand, they may still be at that stage in which they resent all advice and feel that any suggestion made by their parents must be wrong, just because it comes from the parents. This is a typically childish way of behaving, and many grown-ups are still using it. The man who refuses to consider seriously the advice of his parents, or of anyone else; who feels compelled to do the opposite of what is advised, merely in order to show that he is his own boss—that man is just as immature emotionally as the man who is wholly subservient to his parents.

*If Your Parents Feel That They Have Made
Great Sacrifices for You, Look Out!*

I doubt if there is any sure method for reaching a decision on this point, in which your own emotions are so deeply involved; but there is one clue which might be remembered. If your parents have, or *if they think they have*, made great sacrifices for you, then look out. They are likely to claim payment now. After all, they say to themselves, we have done everything for him; we have gone without comforts we should have had, in order to give him a good education. We were glad to make this sacrifice, but surely we are entitled to *some* satisfaction in life. We have not sought this satisfaction in fine clothes or an expensive automobile or a big house; we have been glad to go without all of those for Jim's benefit. All we want is to see him get along well; that is the whole object of our existence; and of course, after all we have done for him, the least he can do for us is to take our advice. Surely that is not very much to ask, since we are right, anyhow!

They will not tell you this in so many words; they will not even say it to themselves; but that is what they will feel. In that case they are interested in themselves more than in you; and you will have to look out for yourself.

In a study [11] of parental advice, it was found that when father and mother differed on the advisability of a marriage, it was safer to follow the father. He was more likely to be disinterested and objective; the mother more likely to be possessive or biased or trying to live her own life over again through her children. The same study also concluded, I regret to say, that the happiest married men are those whose parents are both dead. Being a parent myself, I regard that as one of the most melancholy conclusions in the whole range of modern science. Yet all have known cases in which it was obviously true.

But if your parents are normal persons whom you admire and respect; if they are not appealing to your feeling of gratitude, with sob stories; then you can afford to take their advice very seriously. You cannot afford, merely because it is their advice, to act on it; but you should weigh it long and carefully before you act against it. After all, they probably do have your good at heart; after all, they have lived longer than you have; after all, they might possibly be right.

I skip the obvious, crude cases—those in which a mother has picked out a daughter-in-law who appeals to her and is determined that Sonny must marry the girl, not because *he* loves her but because *she* loves her. That is on a par with the cases (by no means rare) in which the girl's mother proposes to the boy on behalf of her daughter. Take a different type of case, but one that is very common; for instance, the case in which the parents hold strong religious convictions and are anxious that their son should not marry outside the church. Wilbur's parents were energetic Protestants, from a part of the country where the Roman Catholic church is regarded with disfavor by a large part of the population.

Wilbur and Edith met in college and began going together; they had almost reached the point of a betrothal before he learned that she was a Catholic. She did not go to church regularly; but when it came to marriage, of course she would have to be married by a priest; anything else would seem wrong; and, anyhow, her own parents would be shocked. Wilbur did not care particularly how he was married, but he soon realized that this would involve a prenuptial agreement that his children should be brought up as Catholics. It might involve a number of other things that he did not like.

Wilbur and Edith talked it over for months. "Nothing matters except you," each declared. Wilbur agreed that, if necessary, he would be married by a priest; Edith finally declared that, if necessary, she would be married by a justice of the peace. After all, it was their marriage.

Then they told their parents.

Both sets of parents exploded. The question was narrowed down, not to what Edith and Wilbur thought, but to the opinion of their parents. How much weight should they give to such opinion? After all, it was their own marriage, was it not?

Differences in Religion Are More Far-Reaching than You May Suppose.

Everyone has seen such cases. Differences in religion too often are not the problem of the young people, but of others whom they must consider. If they were thrown on a desert island, they would not have the slightest difficulty in coming to an agreement on religion. But unfortunately they are far, far from a desert island. They have to reckon with a lot of difficulties which, they complain bitterly, are not of their own making and correlatively, as they soon recognize, not of their own solving:

1. *The families interfere.* What are you going to do: disown your family? Become an outcast? Break your parents' hearts? Or be forced to follow someone else's judgment rather than your own?

2. *Many other persons interfere.* It is not merely the families, there are all sorts of other relationships to be taken into consideration. There is the priest, or the rabbi, or the practitioner, or your old Sunday school teacher, the Mutual Improvement Association, or the Knights of Columbus, or the Young People's Hebrew Association, or the Ku Klux Klan; there are a score of other influences which are going to be felt, directly or indirectly, not merely now but for years to come. If the parents take a hostile stand, some of these other influences will probably be with them and against you.

3. *Even if you satisfy, or defy, all these influences, there is a broader problem which you may have forgotten;* namely, that these differences of religious faith are not isolated in life but are associated with all sorts of differences that are perhaps more influential.

"When I married Rebecca," George explained to me, "I was not at all worried by the fact that her parents were orthodox Jews. Rebecca and I were more or less freethinkers, anyway; but I respect the Jewish religion as much as any other. Rebecca herself had not been in a synagogue for years. But I overlooked the fact, which I ought to have known, that the Jews represent not merely a religion but a culture. Rebecca could give up the old religious formalities, but she could hardly shake off the entire influence of the culture in which she was reared.

"For instance, I had not counted on the strength of family ties among the Jews; although, if I had been asked about it, I should have told you how much I admired their feeling of family solidarity. My own family had moved west and separated from all its relatives. We never had family reunions in our home—there was no one to reunite. Rebecca's family took me right in as one of themselves; no one could have treated me better than they did personally, in business, in every possible way. A good deal of my success in the automobile business has been due to the fact that her relatives, down to the second and third cousins, began to turn sales my way.

"Since I had no relatives near, it was natural that we should be invited for all holidays, for dinner every Sunday, and for all sorts of other affairs, to the home of Rebecca's parents. They are wonderful people—superior in most respects to mine. But I soon began to feel that I was isolated; I felt like an outsider, no matter how grand they all were to me. They all had things to talk about, that they had been doing and talking about all their lives, and which were good things, but not my things. There was inevitably the same group: Uncle Moe and Uncle Isaac and Uncle Solomon, Aunt Sarah and Aunt Rachel, admirable people all of them; but not my people. They were always reminiscing, always alluding to little family jokes. I was a stranger, even though an honored stranger.

"I felt suffocated.

"When I suggested that we refuse to go to so many Sunday dinners, Rebecca was hurt. 'Why not?' she would ask. 'What excuse have we for hurting their feelings like that? Surely it doesn't harm us to eat a meal once or twice a week with my family. If your family were here, I'd go to their home any time they invited me, naturally.'

"What could I say? Intellectually, I knew that my feeling was wrong; but I'm terribly uncomfortable, nevertheless. The food is not my kind, the conversation is not my kind, the people are not my kind; probably they're all better than my kind; I respect them greatly; but I'm always on the defensive.

"I always prided myself on being intellectually emancipated, and I had not fully realized my unconscious rebellion until our son was born. Rebecca wanted to have him circumcised for hygienic reasons—the doctor advised it. It happens that I myself am not circumcised; although, in the swimming pool at the Y.M.C.A. and in the locker room of the Presbyterian college which I attended, I had occasion to note that a majority of the boys were circumcised. But this became a symbol to me: I could not help feeling, 'They're going to make a Jew out of him.' I burst out into a violent opposition, far beyond the importance of the matter; and Rebecca, of course, let me have my own way. But my violence was a warning to me of my own emotional tensions.

"I adore my wife; and yet, Dr. Popenoe, I sometimes feel like a rat in a trap."

Such was the reaction of an intelligent young man, who found himself drawn into Jewish culture in a great city of Ohio. Rebecca might have felt similarly if she had been plunged into the evangelical atmosphere of a small town in Mississippi.

There are similar differences between the democratic outlook of a Congregationalist or a Unitarian and the authoritarian tradition of a Roman Catholic. Such differences have nothing directly to do with theological beliefs, but they color much of one's outlook throughout life.

4. Moreover, *these differences of all sorts, implanted in earliest childhood, have their roots deep.* They may be disregarded in young manhood, but they crop out later. Husband and wife may be satisfied to have no church affiliations, but worried lest they are making a mistake by not having their own children go to Sunday school. Differences in attitude toward birth control, toward abortion, toward divorce, toward the status of women, may be based not on rational analysis but on the emotionally colored convictions implanted in youth.

After all this has been said—and every reader could document my remarks by cases from his own knowledge —the interesting fact remains that statistically, in a number of studies,[11, 108] there is little or no connection between differences of religious faith or affiliation, and happiness in marriage. The answer to this probably lies in the fact that these studies have been made in regions where religious differences have become less important because religious interests in general have waned. Beyond this, those that marry and remain married long enough to figure in surveys have probably worked out a successful adjustment; they started with attitudes favorable to success.

It is a matter of everyday observation that it is not the religious differences which create friction; it is (apart from the outside influences above mentioned) the attitudes of husband and wife toward these differences. The most extreme combination you can think of —a Mormon and a high-church Episcopalian, or a Unitarian and a hard-shell Baptist, or a Roman Catholic and a Christian Scientist, or any other combination that you may consider highly divergent—may get along perfectly well in marriage because the partners are mature, tolerant personalities, each respecting the other's individuality, and anxious that the other grow along his own lines; while two persons who belong to the same church and have been brought up in it together from the Cradle Roll may split on religious differences because they cannot agree whether they should go to church once on Sunday or twice. It is a matter of personalities and attitudes—apart from the family and other influences.

*Find What the Price Is, and
Pay It in Advance.*

In this complicated situation, I can only give two
general recommendations:

1. *If you want to follow the line of least resistance,*
you may save yourself a good deal of trouble by marrying someone whose religious convictions and affiliations
are, in a general way, like your own. You may thus
avoid the difficulties I have described above, and many
others. The official spokesmen for Protestants, Jews,
Roman Catholics, Latter Day Saints, for almost all
organized religious groups alike, continually urge their
young people not to marry outside the faith.

2. *If, on the other hand, you want to marry outside,*
remember that you will have to pay a price for the
privilege. Find out in advance what the price is; make
up your mind whether you want to pay that price; if so,
pay it in advance and determine that you will not look
backward.

This price may be almost anything. It may be alienation from your own family or alienation of your bride
from hers; it may be giving up your own church to join
hers; it may be the abandonment by each of church
affiliations, and living thenceforward without any association with organized religion; it may be less than any
of these, or much more. Count the price before you go
ahead; and if you want to do so, pay it—in advance.
Do not drift along thinking that maybe something will
turn up to change the situation. Do not make any

promises, half-promises, or hints that you do not intend fully to keep. After that, have enough manhood to stand by your agreement.

In a general way, the argument concerning inter-faith marriages can also be applied, even more strongly, to inter-racial marriages. There are good biological arguments against the mixture of widely different races;[98] but in the personal case it is largely a social problem; it is a question of what your parents will say. You and your wife may get along perfectly well together, but the hostile social pressure is likely to break any except the strongest wills.

What your parents say is a reflection, not merely of their own individual prejudices but of the social world of which they are a part. In such matters they are likely to be the spokesmen for the established order. Hard as it may be for you to admit it, they may often be right in their opinions on your marriage. Take their views into account.

Since marriage is a family affair, the union of two families as well as two individuals, you must get along not only with your own family but also with that of your bride. This involves still more and notoriously difficult problems. A good deal might be said to brides and to mothers-in-law on both sides; and there is a good deal that needs saying, whether or not it would do any good. But so much has already been said about the unwise mother-in-law—who, as often as not, is merely suffering from loneliness and lack of any adequate interests in her life—and sometimes the behavior of the mother-in-law is actually so fiendish, that one forgets the innumerable cases in which the tactful and self-effacing help of the mother-in-law is largely responsible for whatever success the young couple may attain.

On the other hand, a good deal might be said about sons-in-law, who sometimes show little regard for the proprieties: they are childishly tyrannical, feeling that after marriage the bride should no longer know that she has a mother, and acting as if they made themselves more important and superior every time they humiliated the wife's parents. Not to divert the current of my argument unduly, I have relegated to Appendix IV a suggested self-rating scale for sons-in-law. When the time arrives, check up on your own conduct once in a while and make sure that you are consistently headed toward perfection.

To conclude: Young people sometimes resist so energetically the feeling that their parents are trying to influence their choice of a mate that they forget that parental attitudes have two significances: on the one hand, they may represent merely the infantile will to dominance of emotionally warped old people; on the other hand, they may represent the collective wisdom of the race, which has had a good deal of experience with matrimony and knows that young people ruled by "romantic infantilism" are sometimes incredibly silly. The wise course is to give very serious attention indeed, to what your parents say. Weigh it, ponder it, judge it; and in the end make up your own mind, stand on your own feet, and live your own life.

Chapter VII

MARRIAGE IS A FAMILY MATTER

From the first appearance of life on the globe, a chain of descent stretches down, unbroken, to you. If there had been a single link missing in this chain, a million or a hundred million years ago, you would not be here. You are the product of what has gone before; and by your marriage you are taking a share of responsibility for the future evolution of mankind, as well as for your immediate happiness.

What have you to contribute to the future? What has your partner to contribute? Are you fit to marry, fit to have children?

Eugenic fitness is not the prerogative of any small group of self-styled élite. Most of the population is eugenically fit; otherwise it would not be here. Those who have a good average of health, intelligence, and emotional stability are the fit. Usually they come from families that show a good average of the same characteristics.

Those who are marked to a large extent by short life, liability to serious disease, feeblemindedness, or insanity, are open to suspicion, at least. In many instances they will be found to come from families that have more than their share of those undesirable characteristics, with little to offset them. They are below par in eugenical fitness.

Presumably you know something about your own ancestry for at least a couple of generations back. You can easily determine whether you are so far below the average of the population that you ought to eliminate your line from evolution by having no children. If you are fortunate, you may be able to find out something about the family of the young woman in whom you are just now interested. Under the conditions of city life, with a population that is continually moving around (the public utilities companies report that in large cities the average family changes its street address every two or three years), it is often hard to do this, however. Whatever information you can get should be taken into account; not as the only important factor in marriage, but as one of the many important factors that must be weighed unconsciously if not deliberately and, as some would declare, cold-bloodedly.

Most of man's inheritance is made up of normal traits, and these are the ones that should be given special attention. Everyone has a share of the abnormalities and defects—it may be short-sightedness, asthma, or freckles. These are part of his heredity; but so is his breathing and the circulation of his blood.

There are two common but incomplete views of heredity.[66] In one view it is a personal possession of which one may be proud as surpassing the common herd. Just as one has a bigger automobile or more expensive house than the neighbors have, so one may have a better heredity. The other view leads people to shrink and shudder when the word "heredity" is mentioned. It means to them a ghostly hand reaching out of the dead past to blight life's happiest moments, to cut off or drive mad its helpless victim at the height of his usefulness.

No one with even an elementary education in biology will share these fantasies. Heredity must rather be thought of as a condition of life itself, neither extinguishable nor modifiable; as something with which the individual must work, just as he does with gravity. He can annihilate gravity, so far as he is concerned, only by annihilating himself; he can cease to be a part of heredity only by committing suicide. But just as he makes gravity work for him instead of against him, so he makes his heredity useful instead of harmful.

Heredity, then, is neither a cause for invidious pride nor a ground for despair. It is simply a fact to be dealt with. Every child, even the feebleminded one, has more potential talent than is now brought into expression, just as he has also more undesirable possibilities than commonly get into action. Some do carry more handicaps than others; some must face greater abnormalities; but if you, like most people, belong to the great group of the eugenically fit, make it a point not to lose ground when you wed.

The abnormalities that may concern marriage most seriously are conveniently discussed by grouping together those that relate to physical health, intelligence, and emotional stability, respectively.

Physical Abnormalities That May
Affect Your Marriage.

1. *The best general test of physical fitness and resistance to disease is longevity.* No one is immune to all diseases, but a family marked by a high average length of life offers the best possible prospects.[97]

It is unnecessary here to mention the many rare conditions that might be of great importance in special cases. The man in whose family hemophilia or Huntington's chorea runs, is likely to know of it and to be guided accordingly. It is the more commonplace conditions that arouse inquiry, and I shall merely review a number of them very sketchily.

(a) The eye. Defects of this organ are more numerous than any others, in the catalogue of heritable traits. If blindness or serious eye defect runs in the family, get the necessary information from some one who knows.

(b) The ear. The number of persons with impaired hearing is enormous. Congenital deafness is often inherited; and since deaf persons tend to be brought together by sympathy if not by propinquity, marriages between them in the past tended to perpetuate this handicap. It is too great a handicap to be perpetuated, in the opinion of most persons. No one has a right to inflict such a burden on his offspring. Yet there are types of deafness which, though congenital, are not inherited. Do not guess on such an important matter; consult an expert. His verdict is just as likely to surprise you pleasantly as to alarm you. Self-diagnosis is no more to be recommended in problems of hereditary abnormality than in everyday disease. Unfortunately, there are few institutions that are properly equipped to serve the public in such matters; in fact, at the moment of writing I know of none in the United States that is set up for this purpose except the American Institute of Family Relations in Los Angeles. But more will soon be available; and in the meantime a medical specialist, a psychologist, a college biology teacher, or other authority in your neighborhood is almost always glad to help anyone get the best information and advice in such an important matter.

Most serious is the problem of progressive deafness, or otosclerosis. This is inherited according to well-understood rules. It may not make itself manifest to the family until adolescence or even considerably later, but once it starts there is little that can be done to stop it; and too often the man who at marriage is merely "a little hard of hearing" goes on to wear a headphone and finally to be reduced to pencil and paper for communication, becoming a heavy burden to his family. If a woman is afflicted, it is the more grave, because not only may she transmit the defect to her offspring, but each pregnancy is likely to make her own hearing worse.

(c) Asthma and other allergic diseases often run in families, but can scarcely be considered an impediment to marriage except under unusual conditions.

(d) Blood diseases are often hereditary; some of them are extremely serious; but many of them at least can be diagnosed early in life. Various types of anemia need to be taken into account. Pernicious anemia is not only a menace to life but may also lead to mental disturbances. It is hardly necessary to say that the Wassermann or other "blood test", which is required before marriage in many states, has nothing to do with these serious conditions; it is intended merely to discover the presence of syphilis, and is discussed in Chapter XV as part of the pre-marital examination. If there is a history of serious blood disease in the family, look into it.

(e) Heart disease is the commonest cause of death, usually because the heart has worn out, although there may also be an infection, as from syphilis. But some hearts wear out prematurely. Unusually high blood pressure in the family, frequency of apoplexy or paralytic stroke, and similar conditions should be talked over with someone who will be in a position to advise you wisely. A woman with a weak heart must particularly take into account the extra strain of pregnancy.

(f) Diseases of the kidneys are not in the group most affected by heredity, but any kidney defect is potentially serious in women because of the strain on the kidneys during pregnancy.

(g) Skin diseases furnish a long catalogue of inherited peculiarities, but most of them are of little importance in marriage.

(h) Stomach troubles and intestinal and digestive difficulties do not necessarily prohibit a man's marriage; they may be benefited by it through the more regular and better meals that he will get in his own home. Many a bachelor whose inner tube has been tied in knots by a dairy lunch diet has found a quick and enjoyable cure in his wife's cooking. Hereditary factors are of minor importance.

(i) Glandular diseases are numerous and important, and heredity often plays a prominent part. The individual with such a handicap probably knows it and has already sought competent advice. Goiter and cretinism involve the thyroid gland, are amenable to treatment; but the treatment of an hereditary cretin, even though successful, will not change his heredity. Diabetes is associated with a defect of the pancreas and can also be treated successfully, so far as the individual is concerned, without changing his heredity. A man with diabetes may marry under a physician's supervision; a woman with diabetes faces serious difficulties in pregnancy and may have to forego motherhood.

(j) Tuberculosis is so common that it cannot possibly be regarded, of itself, as a bar to marriage; but a low resistance to it is a constitutional factor, and the rare individual who comes from a family that has succumbed to tuberculosis for several generations might be well advised to avoid parenthood if not marriage. One with an active case of tuberculosis should, in most instances, not marry until the disease is arrested, and should be in a position to follow the proper restrictions thereafter. Opinions differ as to the effect of pregnancy on a tuberculous woman. Sometimes she seems benefited during the pregnancy, but has a setback afterward; and most physicians regard active tuberculosis as a strong reason for avoiding maternity.

(k) Cancer offers a subject of unlimited debate to students of heredity. In many instances there appears to be an hereditary pre-disposition; and two persons, both of whom come from unusually cancerous families, should avoid intermarriage. But cancer is too common to be regarded as a serious impediment to marriage, particularly since it is characteristically a disease of the middle years or of old age and therefore cannot be diagnosed or predicted before the wedding.

Intelligence Also "Runs in The Family."

2. *Intelligence* is so desirable in marriage, as in every other walk of life, that few people will be willing to argue about it. However, it exists in every possible degree from the genius to the idiot, and no hard-and-fast line can be drawn between "normal" and "feeble-minded." Every gradation will be found between them.[71] In a general way, dull families produce children who average duller than do the children of bright families. An idiot, however, may be found in a bright family as well as in a feebleminded family, because idiots (or the lowest grades of intelligence in general) are usually the result of some accident of development, and such an accident may occur in any family.[73] The existence of a single very defective child in a family otherwise of high quality is therefore not necessarily a ground

for anxiety. In the absence of expert evidence, the safest policy is to be guided by the general average intelligence of the family for the past two or three generations. A rough measure of this can be had from the amount of schooling the members have taken, the occupations they have followed, and the kind of homes they have maintained.[43] A seemingly bright girl from a stupid family is likely to transmit her family's stupidity, rather than her own brightness, to her offspring.

Emotional Stability and the Tendency to Mental Disease.

3. *Emotional stability* is partly a matter of education, childhood patterns, and experience; but the more serious disorders tend so unmistakably to run in families, and result in such serious maladjustments and breakdowns, that they are properly considered to be among the gravest hindrances to marriage.

The lighter types of emotional instability and immaturity are often called "neuroses." They are a particular menace to marriage because it is often believed by friends and relatives, and even by the victim, that matrimony will be a cure. Marriage is indeed so well adapted to human nature that it benefits most of the people who go into it and sometimes almost works a miracle. But those who depend on it merely for therapeutic purposes are likely not only to disappoint themselves but to ruin the happiness of another.

Take Esther, for instance: everyone agreed that

"Esther is a problem." She was full of fears and conflicts; she was afraid of herself, afraid of sex, afraid of life. Her home was unhappy, as one would expect; and when a casual business acquaintance asked her to marry him, she hardly knew which was the more terrible prospect, going into marriage or staying at home. A violent quarrel with her mother precipitated the castastrophe; she married Godfrey to escape from home, but honestly and desperately determined to do everything in her power to be a good wife. She found on the wedding night that mere conscious determination was not enough to conquer the hidden emotional forces working at cross-purposes with it. After a few months of misery, during which she was a wife in name only, she got a divorce and went back to her mother. Adequate emotional re-education before marriage might have prepared her to be a good wife, but it was a tragedy to go into marriage without such psychological re-conditioning. The time to prepare for successful marriage is long before the wedding ceremony, not afterward—no one seriously asserts the contrary; yet it is incredible how many young people ignore the fact, and how many parents acquiesce in such ignorance.

The serious mental or emotional maladjustments which do not cause a complete breakdown and commitment to a psychopathic hospital usually represent a combination of mental and physical factors [66] —to use the convenient but really meaningless distinction. They run in families to a large extent; and they are often more serious to marriage than insanity, because the neurotic is much more likely to marry than is the person who is nearer to the borderline of incapacitating mental disease.[62] The statistics of divorce (see Chapter VIII) tell something of the price that must be paid for the marriage of thousands of persons each year who had no right to marry until after they had worked out some of their problems of mental hygiene.

Epilepsy is a problem, and a very serious one, too, to several hundred thousand Americans. While it has some tendency to run in families, the genetic basis is uncertain. If an isolated case has occurred in a family that is otherwise superior, it is usually not regarded as a bar to marriage and parenthood, even of those who are closely related. On the other hand, the epileptic man or woman should not marry, much less have children, because of the serious economic and other prospects, and the unfavorable environment for child training. Consult a psychiatrist in any case.

One who has had a real mental breakdown at any time should not consider marriage until after getting the advice of his psychiatrist. Such breakdowns are common: it has been calculated [64] that at some time during life about one American in every ten will break down mentally to the extent of being unable to carry on regular work.

The most serious of the great groups of mental disease, or insanity, is *dementia praecox*, or schizophrenia, a constitutional disorder in which the patient gradually withdraws more and more from activity and falls into a permanent dream-life. Because of this withdrawal tendency, such persons are less likely to marry, and the birth-rate among them is low. The fact that recent methods of treating this disorder have attained unexpected success is no ground for allowing such persons to marry.

What of the person who merely has a parent, grandparent, uncle, or aunt with *dementia praecox?* The disorder "runs in families"; yet even if one parent has it, not all of the children will break down with the same affliction. Statistically, the proportion of offspring who will repeat the parent's symptoms may not be more than 10 per cent or 20 per cent. Some of the other children, however, may be at least "queer." The fact that one has a schizophrenic parent is not necessarily a bar to parenthood, much less to marriage. Judgment would be based on the individual's other characteristics. The best advice possible should be sought for this purpose.

The other great type of mental disease is the so-called "cyclical" type which comprises the manic-depressive psychoses. These are recurrent disturbances, the patient being either highly excited and violent or greatly depressed and sometimes suicidal. These extremes may alternate, but betweenwhiles there may be long periods of relative normality. A man may have had a depression and have recovered. His recovery may continue for the rest of his life; or he may marry and then break down some years later. The manic-depressive woman faces the additional hazard of a breakdown due to the strain of pregnancy. Here again, guesswork is not enough; you may guess to your own disadvantage, and you need the help of a psychiatrist's prediction. It must never be forgotten that there are two sides to the picture. Even though one parent is insane, some of his children may be normal and even unlikely to transmit any handicap themselves. Moreover, some of the elements of mental disease, taken singly, may be valuable; it is when they get into wrong combinations or occur in double doses that they make trouble.

To determine which of an affected parent's children fall into the hopeful, which into the doubtful, class is of course the important task, and one which cannot be tackled with any pretense of complete accuracy of prediction. In fact, complete accuracy of prediction is not part of eugenics. *No one* knows in advance what his own children will be like. Into a superior family with previously flawless record, a defective child may be born. It therefore becomes a matter of statistical, not individual, prediction. It is possible to say that in one case it looks like a ten thousand-to-one bet that the children will be perfectly normal; in another it looks as if the chance of defect was just as great as the chance of normality; it is "even money." Parents must decide for themselves how much risk they are willing to take, since *some* risk is inevitable in life.

Therefore, generally speaking again, the presence of serious mental disease in a family is a reason for going slow. If it exists in the families of both husband and wife, it is worth much more than double consideration. But snap judgment should not be made. Before giving up parenthood, get the best information to be had. Do not guess either for or against yourself in a matter of such importance.

It is true of most inheritable defects—physical, intellectual, or emotional—that if the child gets the same thing from both parents he is likely to suffer more than if he received it from only one. With many defects, the so-called "recessives", one dose may produce no visible result at all; it is only when the same trait is present on both sides of the family that it is immediately dangerous.

Cousin Marriages Demand
Study of Heredity

This furnishes the basis for an answer to the question about cousin marriages,[52] which is asked of us at the American Institute of Family Relations as often as all other questions concerning heredity put together. It is still widely believed that cousin marriages are sinful or dangerous in some way. The prevalent opinion is embodied in legislation, which in half the states makes the marriage of first cousins illegal. Oklahoma extends the prohibition to second cousins.

A study of the customs of other people, past and present, shows that among most of them consanguineous marriage of near degree has been forbidden or regarded as undesirable, and in many instances the fear of resulting defective progeny seems to underlie the prohibition. The tabu may be carried to such excess as in China, where the marriage of two persons with the same surname is forbidden.[55]

On the other hand, it is not difficult to find peoples who make consanguineous marriage a common practice, even in the closer degrees which are now regarded by civilized mankind as incestuous and horrifying.[57] Among the ancient Hebrews, the ancient Egyptians, the ancient Peruvians, and many other sound and vigorous peoples, close unions, even marriages of brother and sister, were regarded as permissible. None of the evil results generally attributed to cousin marriages seems to have been manifested. The consequences more nearly recall the results achieved by livestock breeders, who long ago discovered and applied the fact that close inbreeding is the foundation of all great breeds and families of domestic animals.[30]

Scientifically, the effects of inbreeding are now well understood. They represent merely the union of similar heredities; for, instead of possessing wholly different inherited traits, the mates are, by virtue of their common ancestry, possessors to a greater degree than usual of the same heritable characteristics.

Thus, if the ancestry of the two is good, their children will be benefited by receiving a double dose, so to speak, of certain good traits of their ancestors. On the other hand, in a stock that carries harmful traits, the children are doubly handicapped. However, it often happens that a hidden trait in the family ancestry is brought to light when two related lines of descent are united in a single individual; thus, a feebleminded child may be born in a cousin mating, where feeblemindedness was latent or recessive in the ancestry and had not previously made itself manifest. It is cases like this that have given given consanguineous marriage its ill-repute; although recessive traits may appear disconcertingly in the offspring of unrelated persons, also, if the same trait happens to exist in the ancestry of each.

In passing judgment, therefore, on a proposed marriage, the vital question is not "Are they related by blood?" but "Are they carriers of desirable traits?"

Biologically, then, the marriage of kin may be a good thing or a bad thing. It depends on the kind of germ plasm these kin have received from their progenitors. If the same congenital defect or undesirable trait does not appear in the three previous generations of two cousins, including collaterals, the individuals need not be discouraged from marrying if they want to do so.

But from a broader point of view, the strictly genetic considerations are not the only ones to be weighed in passing judgment on consanguineous marriage. One must also recognize that attachment of cousins sometimes indicates a very narrow circle of acquaintance, a fear of "outsiders", and an undue sentiment for the members of one's own family. It is also evident that two young people are better situated if they have the counsel, help, and influence of two different family circles to fall back on, than if they have only the one in which they were brought up together. On the whole, the individual's interest agrees with that of the race in requiring, at least after the period of adolescence, that his affections be projected out of the home and family in which he was reared.

When Parenthood Should Be Prevented.

In case a man's handicap is such that it affects him only as a possible parent, in case it is quite proper for him to marry provided he does not have offspring, he may have recourse to surgical sterilization to prevent parenthood.[25] The operation of vasectomy requires only a few minutes, is virtually bloodless, and can be performed under a local anesthetic; the man can go about his work almost at once, and his sexual life is not changed in any way except by the prevention of parenthood.[69] A slight incision is made on each side of the scrotum, the slender duct (*vas deferens*) through which the sperm pass is cut and tied, and he is then sterile for life. It is a wholly different operation from castration, in which the testicles are removed and the man thus usually unsexed.[41]

The operation can be undone or reversed later, the tubes being brought together and reunited. However, although this has been accomplished in a number of instances, it is largely a theoretical possibility; it is a delicate operation which few surgeons have attempted, and no one could depend on its success. No man, therefore, should seek sterilization unless circumstances are such that it would never be desirable for him to have a child, even if his first wife should die and he should marry again.

A similar operation, salpingectomy, is performed on women by cutting and tying the fallopian tubes, through which the egg cells pass and in which they are fertilized. This, however, is a major operation, involving the opening of the abdomen. In severity it is about like an operation for chronic appendicitis; it requires a general anesthetic and a couple of weeks in the hospital.[69]

Surgical sterilization is now used in a majority of the American states and in a number of foreign countries [99] to prevent compulsorily the parenthood of persons whose offspring would be likely to be a handicap to all concerned—particularly the insane and feebleminded. It is of great value in this way as a eugenic measure; but this use should not obscure the fact that to the occasional man or woman who must be childless in marriage, it may be an invaluable protection.

A eugenic conscience is highly desirable, but it should not be set on a hair trigger. No one has a make-up or family background in which all the traits are good, none whatever undesirable. At least some are always more valuable than others. A possible handicap should not always be allowed to outweigh a greater probable advantage. It is necessary to strike a balance. Many a conscientious person foregoes parenthood on a very slight chance of handing on to posterity some more or less trivial defect, which might well have been outweighed by the much greater certainty of passing along many and great superiorities.

Those who are counseling in this field agree that when they are consulted as to the desirability of parenthood on eugenic grounds, they usually find the inquirer's scruples to be excessive and parenthood to be recommended. This merely means that those who are intelligent and altruistic enough to be concerned in the matter are usually superior people whose reproduction is socially and eugenically desirable.

Those who marry but must forego parenthood should compensate in some positive and constructive way, either by adopting children or by devoting part of their lives to other people's children—those of the community at large, perhaps. In this way they will have a much better emotional hygiene than if they were merely to sit down and brood over their frustration.

CHAPTER VIII

BEWARE OF WIDOWS, STILL MORE OF DIVORCEES

WHEN old man Weller admonished Sam to "Bevare of vidders," he was not expressing an isolated opinion. Observation shows that there is a widespread tendency on the part of men to be suspicious of widows because, as Alexander Pope put it in some well-known verses, "They are too wise for bachelors to wed." For the same reason, the man who is himself widowed or divorced prefers to marry a woman with no previous experience of marriage.

The fact that only one single man in every thirty-three marries a widow [113] is mainly, however, due to the advanced age of widows, of whom at any given time 88 per cent are over forty years of age.[22] Whether they are wise or not, there are no bachelors for them to wed. If they marry at all, they will marry widowers or, more rarely, divorced men.

Why this prejudice against "wisdom" on the part of a wife?

In the absence of any satisfactory studies of the subject, one must fall back on surmise, supported by the remarks of many men and of folklore and proverbial wit. I suppose that the following factors, among others, influence men more or less unconsciously:

1. *The feeling that the new husband will, after all, be second choice;* that the wife will always be comparing him, to herself if not to others, with the "dear departed" and that, as the latter's vices are forgotten and his virtues magnified under a sentimental halo, his successor may find it impossible to live up to this more or less imaginary record; that he is certain to suffer by contrast. He may even fear that the widow is not marrying him for love at all; that she is still in love with Number One and that she is marrying mainly for convenience—financial, social, sexual, or whatever; perhaps merely to get a father (and supporter) for her first husband's children.

2. *The feeling that widows "know too much" about men;* that they have learned by experience how to manage a man, how to dominate him or "get around" him; that, by virtue of this wifely experience, they have also discarded some of the timidity and reserve that are supposed to be the accompaniments of maidenhood and are willing and able to take advantage of a man's susceptibility to sexual stimulation. A man would like to flatter his vanity by thinking that some woman has fallen in love with his heroic virtues and that it has depended entirely on his own whim to make a conquest of such a subject. It hurts his ego to feel, even unconsciously, that a woman has made an easy conquest of *him,* merely by coming up on his blind side and slipping the halter over his ears.

3. *The feeling that the widow will have formed in her first marriage a sexual pattern,* and that she will try to make him conform to this sexual pattern. Not only may he have an unconscious fear that he cannot conform to this, that she may expect more than he can give, but he feels definitely that it is not his pattern but that of her first husband. He wants to educate her to *his* pattern, thereby keeping the feeling of initiative and sexual dominance which is so important to the average man; and he thinks that this might be a hard job if she has for five or ten years been educated to conform to the pattern of some other man.

One need only state the case in this way for it to appear that there is not much merit in some of these contentions; but I believe that these and similar considerations do help to explain why, as widows so often complain, "I get some propositions but no proposals."

The Widow's Experience May
Be Valuable.

On the other side, it is evident that a woman who has been happily married should be a good prospect for marriage. She is favorably inclined to marriage both in theory and in practice, and she has already passed her apprenticeship in getting along with a man, adjusting herself to the ways of domesticity, and learning something about co-operation in a conjugal partnership. Moreover, if you know something about the facts of her first marriage, you have an invaluable indication of her competence as a home-maker, her interest in a home, her attitude toward family responsibilities; in a general way you have a measurement of all her qualifications for the job. If she has already demonstrated her success, she should not be likely to fail on the second trial.

Appeal may now be made, not to presumptions but to observed cases. I have collected data on 174 men and 158 women, all educated Americans, who remarried after the death of the previous partner. The happiness of these remarriages was rated by close friends and relatives as follows:

	Happy	Doubtful	Unhappy	Total
Widowers	102	42	30	174
Widows	76	46	36	158

A majority of these remarriages (59 per cent in each sex) turned out to be definitely happy. The widowed man has apparently no advantage over the widowed woman. The percentage of happiness does not differ greatly from that of the average run of marriages in the educated part of the population.

From these figures as well as from common sense, one is justified in concluding that the question whether the young woman is a widow is not of primary importance. The main question is whether she is emotionally mature. If she is one of those emotionally infantile females who cannot adjust herself to bereavement, who must always be true to the memory of her Great Romance—who is going through life as the bride of a ghost, in other words —you may well beware of her just as you would beware of a maiden with similar defective emotional hygiene. But if you yourself are mature enough not to be stampeded by anyone, you will judge the widow on her merits, not on your own lack of self-confidence.

It will still be the case, however, that most widows are unable to remarry, if for no other reason than their age. Everyone who has to do with problems of marriage is continually getting letters from strangers, which start something like this: "Dear sir:—I am a widow of sixty (though my friends all say I don't look a day over fifty), and I am wondering whether there is not somewhere a good Christian gentleman with means enough to support a wife, who, etc., etc., etc." The answer is No.

The situation of the divorced woman, with respect to remarriage, is better than that of the widow only in that she is usually younger.[22] At any given time, 59 per cent of all divorced women are under forty and 37 per cent under thirty. In every other respect, her prospect is less favorable, because she has already failed once in the most important enterprise of life. The burden of proof is on her to show that she was not to blame; or, if she was to blame, that she has learned her lesson, expensive though that type of education may be; and that with a different husband she will be, if not all that could be desired in a wife, at least all that any reasonable man has a right to expect.

There Is Rarely an "Innocent Party"
in a Divorce Case.

But if she declares that she was not to blame in the failure of the first marriage, she will have to face the obvious fact that it takes two to make a marriage; that it takes two, proverbially, to make a quarrel; and that it takes two to destroy a marriage. There are, of course, some exceptions. Occasionally a partner may go insane, or "take to drink" (even though not driven to it by the spouse), and become a problem that no human being could expect to solve. But it is high time to get rid of the old idea that there are two parties to a divorce, the innocent one and the guilty one. Unfortunately, some laws and religious canons recognize this distinction, allowing the "innocent party" to a divorce to remarry, but not the guilty one. Yet the most superficial investigation will show how hard it is to find a really innocent party to a divorce. What the laws consider is that one party has committed adultery and the other is not known to have done so. This makes the first one guilty, the second innocent. It is no condonement of adultery to declare that there are plenty of other crimes which can be committed against marriage. The "innocent" wife may have committed all of these crimes against marriage except one; nevertheless she is innocent, and the husband whom she has sometimes almost forced into adultery is guilty. The fact that three fourths of the divorce suits are brought by women certainly does not mean that in three fourths of the cases the man is more to blame than the woman. The argument is the same when the sexes are reversed: a husband who is technically innocent in one respect, but no other, may be much more to blame for destroying the marriage than is the wife against whom his detectives finally get evidence of infidelity.

Most divorces, of course, are not granted on the ground of adultery, but on grounds of cruelty, desertion, and similar misbehavior. It is not human nature for divorced persons afterwards to say, "It was mainly my own fault." Some do say it; and a recent study [105] revealed that of all divorced persons interviewed, 25 per cent admitted they would like to remarry the former partner. Many others undoubtedly wished they could, even though they would not admit it; and some divorcees do remarry [95] each other—four or five times! But, in any event, neither party to a divorce is ordinarily wholly free from the responsibility of failure —too often a sordid and degrading failure. This is the first reason to beware of divorcees.

The second is their low average of inherent fitness, biologically. Unless one has studied the figures,[77] it is hard to believe what a bad showing divorcees make. They are three or four times as likely to become insane,[126] to commit suicide, and to be sent to prison, as are married persons of the same age; and their expectation of life is scarcely more than half as good.[114] Add to this the high degree of sterility [85] they show (since the majority of them are childless, even though they have on the average been married for nearly ten years before divorce),[12] and one has a picture of biological inferiority, largely constitutional in character, and of a sort that is not easily remedied.[39] Anyone seeking a wife (or husband) among persons with such a large average degree of inferiority is of course looking for the exceptions; but he must look with caution.

The third reason for considering divorcees carefully is the difficulty they have in making adjustments after divorce, and the additional damage often done to the personality by these difficulties.[122] The divorcee, having had trouble in marriage, thinks naïvely that she will solve her difficulties by terminating the marriage. Divorce, however, is not a solution of difficulties but a running away from them. If the difficulties are inside the unhappy woman, then she merely takes them along with her as she runs; and at the same time she is running into a new set of difficulties which may be even harder to solve than those from which she tried childishly to escape by abandoning her marriage. It cannot be repeated too often that those who succeed in marriage face the same difficulties as do those who fail. The difference is that the first-named solve their problems,* the latter run away from them.

The readjustments which the divorced person must make are often beyond the capacity of the victim and

---

* Because the two persons concerned are so deeply involved emotionally, it is often necessary for them to get outside help to view their situation objectively. Taking advice from friends and relatives is likely to do more harm than good.[123] In a large proportion of cases a scientific counselor with even a moderate amount of skill and experience can show the couple how to solve their problems, if they want to do so.

lead to insanity or suicide. In other cases they are made successfully at the cost of an effort which, if it had been applied to the marriage rather than to the divorce, would have made the marriage successful. Think of the new problems which the divorcee has to face: an adjustment to the loss of ideals, of self-esteem, of self-confidence, sometimes of self-respect; a reformation of innumerable little habits of daily life; an adjustment to a changed social life (or sometimes to the lack of any); a complete change in sexual expression; a financial problem which is often extremely difficult for the woman, and at least onerous for the man. If children are involved, as is the case in nearly a third of the divorces, there are additional heartbreaks. No wonder, in such straits, that divorced persons do a lot of things which make trouble for themselves and others.[81]

Widowed persons have to make some, though not all, of the same readjustments. The difference in the death-rate, the rate of suicide, insanity, and imprisonment, between the widowed and the divorced therefore helps to give one an idea of how much of the divorcee's trouble is merely a consequence of the break-up of the home, and how much to other factors, either emotional or constitutional. The two can be matched sex for sex and age for age. In every respect, those widowed by death make a better showing than do those widowed by law.

Most Divorcees Do Not Remarry.

With such a large amount of biological inferiority and emotional immaturity as one finds among divorcees considered as a class,[68] it is evident that their rate of remarriage will not be high. Here again one may be misled by newspaper accounts of the remarriage of divorcees, until he supposes that a large part of the people who get divorces do so in order to marry someone else, in the pattern of serial polygamy that is characteristic of a few circles in the United States. It can be said with a good deal of confidence that this is not a general pattern. Much more frequently, people go through the divorce court merely because they have never learned how to face life in an adult manner and therefore follow the neurotic pattern of running away, meanwhile thinking up a lot of apparently plausible reasons for doing so. If they do get divorces with the expectation of marrying someone else, they are often disappointed.

For a variety of reasons it is impossible to ascertain the exact number of divorcees in the population. Many of them misrepresent their status to the census enumerator as well as to the public. It seems probable, however, that an actual majority of all those who get divorces never remarry. Of those who do remarry, men preponderate; the age factor, as well as the man's preference for marrying a virgin, again works against the woman. What is the success, on second trial, of those who do achieve remarriage? The following table presents the data of 4,694 cases that I have accumulated over a period of years, the happiness being rated by close friends and relatives:

	HAPPY	DOUBTFUL	UNHAPPY	TOTAL
Divorced men	1,259	577	629	2,465
Divorced women	1,168	447	614	2,229

It appears that the minority of divorcees who do succeed in remarrying have about half a chance of success at the second attempt. The exact percentages are fifty-one for the man, fifty-two for the woman.

In a group marked by average biological inferiority, some are of course much inferior to others, and these are the ones who end up in prison, in a mental hospital, or in the grave.[45] On the other hand, in such a great body of persons (increased each year by nearly half a million more who are ground out of the divorce mill) there are innumerable admirable persons. The low quality of the average must not obscure the fact that there is in this tragic procession much good material; many superior persons who, through ignorance, foolishness, lack of effort, or misadventure, have been thrown out of their homes by a collision; for failure of marriage does not result from some special combination of traits, but from a collision of wishes. These superior persons should have a chance to remarry; and if a superior person has in some way made the mistake of marrying one who is highly inferior, it is to his advantage, and socially desirable, that he have a chance to rectify this mistake by a second marriage. Men can take advantage of this opportunity in many instances and have a fifty-fifty chance of attaining in a second marriage that happiness which they did not achieve in the first. Women have the same chance if they can find a second partner; but the age factor added to other handicaps prevents most of them from finding an opportunity to remedy the first mistake.

One can say of the divorced, therefore, as of the widowed, that it is not the mere fact of divorce which is to be considered; it is the personality of the divorcee. The figures tell all too plainly the average inferiority of divorcees, whether male or female, and double care should therefore be used.

CHAPTER IX

AND ABOVE ALL, BEWARE OF BOGUS ROMANCE!

MANY marriages are based on the Romantic Platform, of which half a dozen planks can be recognized easily enough by anyone who gets his education for marriage from the usual sources; that is, from the movies, the radio crooners, the billboards, the newspaper headlines, the wood pulps, and the women's slick magazines:

1. *Love is a mysterious visitation.* It comes out of the nowhere into the here; unexpected, unannounced, perhaps uninvited. It is unpredictable, uncontrollable, undependable. No one knows whence it comes; all that anyone can possibly know is that it has come. (The man who knows that much knows something!) You are going down the street, pondering on the future of the League of Nations. You turn a corner, or you step into an elevator, or an automobile crashes in your front yard. Your Psychological Moment steps out and looks you in the eye, and then *it is on.* A moment ago it was not on; now it is; that is all there is to it. That is all you can ever know about it.

In moments of disillusion and despair, when faith withers away and there seems to be no meaning in the universe, a man may admit to himself that not all love is

love at first sight. Even from such depths of despond-
ency, he will probably beware of making such a confession to his wife. If it is not fully settled that he fell in
love with her at first sight, he is always on the defensive,
always trying to explain what was the matter with him,
always asserting that she does not understand, that he
really and truly did fall in love with her at first sight
but was afraid to admit it—she seemed so ethereal, so
incredible, so inaccessible, that he simply did not dare to
avow the emotion which overwhelmed him.

2. *Once this mysterious visitation has come into your
life in this unpredictable and unascertainable manner, it
is so important that you are justified in giving up everything else to cultivate it.* No sacrifice can be too great
for that purpose. A man is justified in giving up his
wife. A woman is justified in giving up her home and
children. A king is justified in giving up his throne.
Anyone is justified in giving up anything to cultivate
Romance when it has thus arrived unannounced and un-
attended. It is a duty of a profoundly sacred kind. He
cannot be true to his inmost nature, to his better self,
if he hesitates for one moment in the face of this call.
If he stops to count the cost, he is a niggardly and mer-
cenary wretch, a callous and cold-blooded fool, a spirit-
ual mummy whose soul has shriveled up into a peanut
shell.

3. *The third plank in the Romantic Platform is that
Love is a mysterious visitation in both a positive and a
negative sense*: that is, it may go as unpredictably as it
came. Nobody is very much surprised when it goes.

Even though every boarding-school girl knows at least one quotation from Shakspere, "Who ever loved that loved not at first sight?", it is known esoterically that these episodes are not always as permanent as they ought to be.

"I fell in love with Howard at first sight," Loretta reminisces.

"Why didn't you marry him, then?"

"Oh, I saw him a second time, later on," she explains.

Since Love is uncontrollable in its goings as well as its comings, there is nothing you can do about it. Yesterday the sky was clear, the sun was shining, the fire of Love was burning brightly in your heart. When you awake today, you discover that the sky is overcast, the sun has disappeared, and that the flame has flickered out. That is all there is to it. You know that you cannot get fire out of dead ashes, cannot produce heat from cold cinders. All that you can do is to be a realist; to recognize that it was an interesting episode while it lasted, but that no one in his senses expects such things to last forever. That chapter is finished.

4. *However, while one episode is finished, another may come along and take its place.* It is the very essence of Romance that you may have a long series of such supreme experiences. You may be a two-time loser, or a three-time loser, or any other number that appeals to your imagination. Some ambitious young men have even raised the question whether it is not possible to love two girls at the same time. The answer is, "Not if the girls find it out." But, at least, Father Time and Mother

Nature may be hoped, if not absolutely counted on, to make good your loss. You close the gold-illumined pages of the Book of Love; you lay Youth's Sweet-Scented Manuscript back in the top bureau drawer; and you start off down the street again to attend to the problem of the League of Nations, which you have so long neglected for more important affairs. But lo! you turn another corner, or you step into another elevator, or an airplane crashes in your back yard; another Psychological Moment steps out and looks you in the eye; you recognize the same cardiac-respiratory phenomena that you experienced the first time: and all you know is that *it's on again*.

5. *The fifth plank in the Romantic Platform is that each of these supreme affairs is just as supreme as each of the others*. It would be absurd to say that you loved Jeanne more than Jeannette and less than Jeanneton. You love them all just as much as you can, which, if you do say so, is a considerable amount. Each is just as divine as every one of the others; and vice versa. Jeanne is incomparable, Jeannette is indescribable, Jeanneton is unbelievable; but Jane is also inconceivable, Joan unsurpassable—and Janice is yet to come.

A Good Deal of Supposed Romance is Nothing But Infantile Self-love.

It follows that you actually do not love any of these lovely creatures for what they are. Whatever Love means (which is nothing at all, as I shall point out in the next chapter), it must have some relation to the welfare of the loved one. But when you are thus caught up in the fiery cloud and carried to heaven on the wings of Romance, you are not particularly concerned about the fulfillment of the personality of the beloved. You are not sacrificing yourself to plan for her future. Perhaps she is like the Rose of Washington Square in a once popular song: "She has no future, but oh, what a past!" You are not devoted to her past, either—that is over. As for her present, you may be destroying what yesterday was her whole world; but it is All for Love, and the World Well Lost. The only thing in the world that really matters is your love; and that is a subjective sensation. It is this sensation that becomes, for you, the Greatest Thing in the World. Nothing is important now except the sensation that Jeannette creates in your overworked heart. Of course you would not say that at one time you did not love Jeanne just as much; she was sensational, too—but why drag that in? Of course, such things cannot last. It is not so important *whom* you love, as that you love *someone*. Jeannette is simply marvelous; and though there have been some evidences that she, too, might vanish with the rose, you already have an eye on Jeanneton, and you will know where to turn next. A Great Lover is not easily discouraged.

In short, you do not value any of these priceless creatures for what they are, but merely for what they do to you, for the effect that they produce on you; which brings up

6. *The last and inescapable plank in the Romantic*

Platform. Actually you did not love any of these charmers at any time; all that you loved was yourself! Another song, popular a hundred years ago, stated it succinctly: "I love the girls for loving me, but I love myself the best!"

In its extreme form, which I have been caricaturing here (but in the last half a dozen motion pictures you saw, were not some of the planks of the Romantic Platform presented sympathetically several times?) the whole Romantic Complex is nothing but Romantic Infantilism—the infant's self-love dressed in grown-up clothes, with some Hollywood stage-settings, and trying to make a child's game out of the most serious adult responsibility of life. Of course it fails. Of course people who marry for Romance, with no more education for marriage than they have derived from the movies and the wood pulps, or from the whisky baritones and cocktail contraltos of the air-waves, are likely to end up in the divorce court—if they do not end up in slaughter and permit the newspapers to headline another Love Murder or Love Suicide.

The Romantic Platform is the support of other important features of the contemporary marriage. One of these is the Great Lover. So much has this rôle been publicized by the popular educational agencies I have mentioned, that it would be hard to find a man in the United States who, if he were honest, would not admit that he secretly cherishes the ambition to be a Great Lover.

Unfortunately, his patterns are usually wrong. In

particular, he is misled by propaganda to the effect that American men are only second-rate lovers; that the Europeans excel in this fine art; and that the American who wishes to succeed must follow a continental pattern.

What are the facts as to European "lovers"? Some European males, like some American males, have learned to do a considerable amount of posing, bluffing, lying, and doublecrossing in order to gratify their *self-love*. The performance of such a male has about as little to do with love as the whistle of the engine has to do with pulling the train. Its main purpose is to inflate the man's ego by giving him a cheap feeling of power.

Without ascribing this type of "love" to a whole nation, one may reasonably take a look at the European vital statistics. There are few European countries that do not have a higher rate of infection with venereal diseases than the United States and, so far as can be judged in the absence of reliable statistics, a higher abortion rate. The suicide rate among young women who have been favored with attention from these Great Lovers sometimes reaches heights quite unknown in America. The illegitimate birth-rate in many European countries is not only much higher than among whites in the United States, but even much higher than among American Negroes.

If all these conditions reflect the superior erotic culture of the European male, the United States may well be satisfied with its provincial bourgeois ignorance!

From a scientific point of view it is clear that this

self-proclaimed type of European "lover" has no more relation to love than the "protection" which racketeers extend to small merchants through blackmail and terrorism has to do with a genuine and legitimate protection. Europe has no monopoly on infantile auto-eroticism, either male or female; but it is certainly not necessary to import any of it into this country as a rare luxury.

While Romantic Infantilism creates, among other nuisances, the Great Lover delusion among men, it is also largely responsible for the Glamour Girl. Since the girl's success in creating a sensation in the heart of the man is, on this platform, not dependent on her durable and permanent qualities, but merely upon superficial impression, everything is sacrificed to the impression. "Save the surface and you save all" was a slogan once adopted by paint manufacturers to sell their products. The Glamour Girl has adopted it as the Law of Life.

Whenever the value of the package is greater than the value of the contents, one may diagnose the case as "glamour." The president of a woman's college complains that the modern girl is "too vogue on the outside and too vague on the inside." That is precisely the Glamour Girl: pretty as a picture—overexposed and underdeveloped.

The merchant who sells inferior goods by wrapping them in a fancy package is selling them on glamour. Why does he try to sell his merchandise on glamour? Naturally, because he has strong doubt as to the real value of the merchandise, but a strong desire to sell it regardless.

One of the tragic features of marriage today is the one-sided emphasis on such superficialities as a "school-girl complexion", "romantic allure", the seductiveness of mystery and inaccessibility. Such things are continually represented to young women as being the stuff of which happiness in marriage is made. Of course they are mostly good in their proper place and in due proportion, but it is not humanly possible for anyone to base a permanently successful marriage on those alone.

Genuine Romance Has an Important Biological Function.

When one extracts from Romance the infantilism which creates Great Lovers and Glamour Girls, it is evident that there must be an important residue of some sort. An ideal which has such compelling power in life must have something back of it. I think one can distinguish three different elements in the substance that is left after the pure infantilism is squeezed out of Romance:

1. *The romantic ideas of the adolescent period have largely colored the whole use of the term.* In most instances, it appears that the middle-aged person who is seeking romance is in reality seeking a return to adolescence.

If one collects the ideas of romance expressed or unexpressed by high school girls, a fairly definite picture emerges, even though the outlines are blurred. At this stage, romance seems to consist largely of illusion, fantasy, unreality. Youth becomes aware of the world in which it must live, and is not satisfied with that world. The attempt to remake the world—to "remould it nearer to the heart's desire"—is not likely to be successful in practice. The simplest way to attain satisfaction is to imagine one's self in an unreal world which can be shaped into any form that youth prefers. In such dream-world, the girl finds a type of satisfaction which reality seldom yields.

2. *Passing beyond this concept of romance to a little more advanced age, it appears that romance is to a large extent that which is emotionally stimulating.* The emotions concerned are those associated with sex, in most instances.

3. *For another idea of romance,* one may turn to the literary critics. The world's fiction has been classified as either realistic or romantic. If one seeks a definition of these terms, realism is found to deal with things that are common or usual; romance with the unusual. The unusual is naturally more stimulating to the emotions, simply because it is unusual. There are of course many limitations and qualifications in literary theory and artistic practice, but the distinction just drawn appears to be the general basis of differentiation.

If one attempts to generalize from these concepts, it will be seen that the idea of romance has a sound biological basis. This involves, first, a satisfaction of innate dispositions, especially those connected with sex as distinguished from those associated mainly with the herd or the ego; and second, the avoidance of monotony in the satisfaction of these dispositions.

The effect of monotony is just as pronounced physiologically as it is psychologically. Repetition of the same stimulus brings a steadily decreasing response, in accordance with one of the most familiar of biological laws (Weber's Law). To maintain a level of response, still more to increase it, one must have continually stronger and stronger stimuli. Since the usual soon becomes commonplace and monotonous, the unusual must be sought for increased satisfaction.

From this point of view, romance might be defined as "a search for variety among pleasurable stimuli, especially those with more or less remote sexual coloring." Obviously, it serves a useful purpose; indeed, perhaps a necessary purpose in adjusting the individual to life.

When harm results from the search for romance, it is due to false romance; that is, romance which involves impossible or harmful situations. One addicted to cocktails or cocaine is seeking essentially the sort of satisfaction that the school girl finds at the movies. It is an escape from reality: a rejection of the actual environment, and the creation in its place of an imaginary one which is less exacting or more exciting.

This adolescent type of romance is, except in small quantities, injurious because it antagonizes an understanding of reality and leaves the individual less able to meet the problems of daily life. How far indulgence in fantasy is a normal or useful occupation, is a matter of some debate; but even with the most lenient view of the situation, a danger-line must be recognized.*

It is not necessary to enlarge on the undesirability of harmful stimuli, whether they tend to the impairment of the personality or to anti-social actions. Excluding them, romance appears to be a normal and useful ingredient in life. There is no intrinsic reason why everyone should not seek a reasonable amount of romance as long as he lives.

If romance is to occupy its proper place in life, the first thing to do is to define it properly and to strip from it the infantile components. Then and only then will it be possible to consider seriously the ways in which the amount of romance in the world may be increased and a proper supply of it assured to every adult.

Since no two people have the same idea of romance, it follows that no two people can be satisfied in just the same way. The basal patterns of romance are widespread and, if one takes them at a low enough level, probably universal. But the actual forms are enormously colored by culture. Comparing the idea of romance of an upper-class girl in feudal Japan with that of an upper-class girl in modern Hollywood, one would be struck mainly by the dissimilarities. The underlying

* A good deal of daydreaming is to be expected in adolescence. Later, it is justifiable only if it does not take too much of one's time, and if it meets the following requirements: (1) it must not be a substitute for activity; (2) it must deal with socially acceptable activities—not with vice or crime; (3) it must deal with activities that could be put into effect— not complete impossibilities; and (4) the subject must then go ahead and try to put these ideals into effect. In such a case, daydreaming is transformed from mere fantasy into creative imagination.

resemblances might become visible only after some analysis.

In the modern sense, romance is a relatively recent discovery of the western world. It is an exotic importation, borrowed by the Crusaders from Arabic and Persian sources less than a thousand years ago, and developed by the troubadours. One will seek far in Greek and Roman literature for even a germ of the idea of romantic love which is found full-grown in the *Arabian Nights* and which, since the Crusades, has been so popularized in occidental civilization that it is now hard to believe it has not always existed.

Possibly such ideas of romantic love could arise most easily in a civilization where women were segregated from the cradle and where men had to depend on imagination and fantasy instead of on coeducation for an understanding of "the kindly species"—to borrow the Arabic equivalent of "the fair sex." If this is true, then it is easy to see that there might be difficulties in maintaining such a romantic attitude toward sex in a civilization where women associate more freely with men.

With this conflict between traditional romantic fantasy and the reality of daily contact with the other sex, it might be expected that romance and reality would clash continuously. There would be two natural outcomes: on the one hand, disillusionment and cynicism; on the other hand, a refusal to admit defeat and a greater and greater reliance on fantasy, along with a desperate effort to transmute reality into forms that satisfied fantasy. Are not both of these results traceable in the confused gropings of young people today toward a code of sex ethics?

A scientifically based plan of life must find a place for romance; but this romance must be of a type that is attainable, that is usable, and that will increase the efficiency of the user instead of leading him into disaster.

Success depends on respecting the biological bases. Seeking to avoid monotony and boredom, one might try to proceed along either one of two different lines:

In the first place, the amount of stimulus can be increased continually in order to prevent response from decreasing. This is the line usually chosen (e.g., in petting and necking) and is, of course, self-defeating, since it is impossible to increase any stimulus indefinitely. There must come a time when either the possibility of increase will be exhausted, or the subject will be exhausted. One who derives emotional stimulus from music, for example, cannot increase indefinitely the amount of music heard. There is always a limit imposed by the fact that there are only twenty-four hours in a day, not to mention other obvious limitations. The common attempt, then, to enrich life by increasing the intensity of emotional stimuli, is largely in the wrong direction.

A sounder policy would be to vary the stimulus and thus evoke a different response. When music ceases for the moment to charm, one turns to other arts.

A misunderstanding of this plan is responsible for a great deal of unhappiness in the world. Considering his wife monotonous, a man seeks a different stimulus by going to some other woman. But actually, he is getting the same sort of stimulus that he received from his wife when they first married; it is therefore nothing new but merely more of the same. The more he seeks stimulus from a variety of women, the more he gets the same superficial response, because no woman can give to a relative stranger anything more than a superficial knowledge of her personality. It is only in a lifelong partnership, in which the depths of personality can be explored, and the many different and continually changing aspects of it discovered, that one has the opportunity for a real growth of experience. The attempt to substitute for this a mere extension of superficial experiences, as in promiscuity, not only is self-defeating but is almost certain to lead the man back to an infantile level of self-gratification. The man whose emotional equipment is thus limited to self-gratification will never be able to live fully and to profit by the exploration of the inexhaustible depths of a woman's personality, with the continual new and unexpected interests these present, because such depth of experience is possible only with emotional security and growing trust, confidence, and self-revelation, such as monogamy creates.

So far as sex is concerned, then, the bogus Romance of the movies is a common barrier to full satisfaction in marriage. Romance is to be sought not in infantile philanderings but in adult life-partnership that is being continually deepened, enriched, and transformed as the two partners continually change each other.

In other aspects of life, romance is to be sought by an enrichment of the daily process of living in a greater variety of ways—more intellectual and artistic interests, more creative outlets, more variety in social contacts, more variety in the routine of daily living, more variety in exercise—more outdoor life, sunshine, fresh air, and water. When people take romance seriously as a biological problem, they will devote as much attention to the management of romance in daily life as they now devote to the management of finance. By so doing, they will be likely to avoid the infantile and disintegrating elements that are now too often attached to the idea of romance; and they will enrich their own lives greatly in the process.

CHAPTER X

NOW, ARE YOU *REALLY* IN LOVE?

SHE is a nice girl and all that, but how can you be sure that you really *love* her?

How could you be sure that you loved anybody?

What is love, anyway?

Merely a word; a word which does not mean the same to any two persons; a word, therefore, which, from a scientific point of view, means nothing.

Keep it for use in a hammock under the June moon. For the present discussion it will be necessary to stand on firmer ground. What is the relationship which holds a man and woman together in permanent bond, with the highest values that human experience can find? I suggest that it be called the Primary Sex Complex, merely to get a term that does not start with too many meanings. The Primary Sex Complex consists of five elements, all of which must be present if you are to get out of life all that you desire.

Look for Five Elements of the
Primary Sex Complex.

1. *The biological mating impulse.* This is fundamental, it dates back to the most primitive times, and it

is unnecessary to emphasize its importance. But it is far less important than is sometimes supposed. It is too transitory to serve as the basis of a permanent marriage; and historically it was not the foundation of marriage and family life.

There could be no greater error than to identify this biological mating impulse with human love, and the tendency to make this error vitiates a large part of the so-called "radical," and destructive, writing on marriage and the family during the past generation. As a biologist, I should be the last to dispute the importance of it; yet there are innumerable successful marriages in which the biological mating impulse has largely died out; a few even in which it was never present recognizably.

I put it first; but it is only the beginning of the story.

2. *The economic relationship* growing out of the division of labor between man and woman has been more important, in many ways, in the creation of the monogamous family. It is a product of the specialization of the female for childbearing, and it would be important as far back as one can imagine the course of prehistory. During a large part of her life, the woman was handicapped to some extent by the process of childbearing and child rearing—handicapped for defending herself from enemies, and for getting out and rustling food. It was therefore a great advantage to her to have an able-bodied male who would protect her at these times; who would bring in the food for all of them.

Conversely, it was an advantage to the man, absent

on hunting or fishing or fighting expeditions, to have some one at home to protect the stored-up food supply, prepare for the future, and keep the home fires burning. It is hard to realize, in modern civilization, how important was the last-named task in primitive times when mankind first learned to control fire—hundreds of thousands of years ago. It was not easy to replace the fire if it died out; it might be a matter of life and death to keep the fire burning. Someone had to stay close to the hearth for that purpose; and since the woman was kept more inactive, during part of the time, by the care of small children, the task naturally fell to her while the larger and stronger male, biologically better equipped for activity by spurts, took over the hunting and fighting expeditions. Thus a division of labor was so natural as to be inevitable. It was to the advantage of all concerned. It brought about the economic relationship which made man and woman dependent on each other, each complementing and supplementing the other, neither complete without the other—a relationship that is as true and important economically as it is physically.

So long as women bear children and men do not, woman will have to be economically dependent on someone outside herself during a part of her life. She may depend either on her own husband, or on the community. Some feminists have felt that they were degraded and humiliated by being dependent on their own husbands, and have argued that they would prefer to be dependent on the taxpayers in general through "endowed motherhood" or something of the sort. Psychologically there seem to be good reasons for believing that a man will work harder for his own family than he will for anyone else's family. While the economic dependence of women has been greatly modified in the course of evolution, it has in one way become more important rather than less. The child of modern man has a longer period of dependence than does the offspring of lower animals. He thus requires longer care, either from his mother or from some other woman. Again, there are good reasons for believing that on the average a mother will do better by her own children than she will by the children of the neighbors.

The fact that the modern girl may have a job before marriage and may continue this job indefinitely after marriage, should not prevent recognition of this fundamentally necessary division of labor which has created the intricate and reciprocal relationship between man and woman in marriage. Better education will lead to a better management of this relationship, men discarding a patriarchal tradition and women abandoning the neurotic feelings about home-making which some of them now cultivate.

From an evolutionary point of view, woman is well adapted to what is still the principal work for most women, namely, home-making; while man is not at all well adapted to what has become his principal work, namely, participation in business or industry. He is biologically better adapted to spurts of activity with periods of rest between; and is motivated largely by a self-assertive and combative disposition, which is not well controlled until he becomes more mature emotionally than are most men. Consequently he tends to turn his business and industry into a fight, whether it be as a capitalist or as a labor union organizer. Agriculture is in most respects better suited to his inherent nature than are some of the other things which occupy his time; but in general he is something of a fish out of water, with less opportunity in modern society to find satisfaction for his innate tendencies than has his wife.

3. *A third factor in the Primary Sex Complex is what may be called sexually colored comradeship*—comradeship in the sexual sphere. By this I mean the tenderness and affection which exist between husband and wife; the advantages of having someone who sees the best in her partner rather than the worst, as his competitors have been doing all day long; of having someone who helps the partner to deepen and enrich his personality, instead of trampling it under foot, as his competitors do all day long; all those precious elements which may be summed up as emotional security.

This sexually colored comradeship, this tenderness and affection, this emotional security, are so valuable that they are often described as "love." They persist year after year and may become deeper, richer, and stronger, long after the biological mating impulse has died out. They are popularly supposed to be derived from the biological mating impulse, but there is little ground for such a derivation. The biological mating impulse is largely a self-regarding thing, sometimes brutal. The "tender emotion", which is rudimentary among animals below man in evolution, probably derives more from the mother-child relationship than from the biological mating impulse. The man has been brought into the mother-child relationship very gradually; he has, in a word, been domesticated. The process is by no means complete. To the extent that man assumes the full responsibilities of a husband and father, he is civilized and in the line of evolutionary progress.[120] The man who wants to "love 'em and leave 'em" is not merely infantile in his emotional development but, from an evolutionary point of view, is a throwback to a level which would make a chimpanzee grin with derisory self-esteem.

4. *A fourth element in the Primary Sex Complex is non-sexually colored comradeship,* or comradeship in the non-sexual sphere. By this I mean the intellectual companionship a man might have with another man; but, if this companionship is with a woman, it is doubled in value because now he sees everything not merely through the eyes of an intelligent companion but through the eyes of a companion who, because she is of the other sex, will see everything differently and thereby increase his interest in the exchange of views.

In practice this non-sexual comradeship cannot be wholly isolated; there is at least an unconscious recognition that the partner is of the other sex. It is the most recent of the elements that make up the Primary Sex Complex. While it could doubtless be discovered in a rudimentary form far down the scale, its development as a keen and active appreciation of the personality, individuality, and uniqueness of the partner is a fairly recent achievement, which many men have not yet made.

5. *The final element in the Primary Sex Complex is the mutual interest in home and children.* This again goes back to the most primitive period. It is this along with the economic interest ("2" above) which, working together, are mainly responsible for building up monogamous marriage and the modern family with all its values.

Since these elements have come into the picture at different times from different sources, they are not indissolubly linked together. The Primary Sex Complex can be broken up. To the extent that it is broken or reduced, the bond which holds man and woman together is less significant, less valuable.

To the question "How can I tell when I am really in love?" a common answer is: "When the real thing comes along, you won't have to ask—you'll know it without being told." This is mere nonsense. In the preceding chapter I have pointed out how illusory and dangerous it is to be guided by mere subjective feelings. The feelings are legitimate, and desirable as well as enjoyable; but anyone who puts his whole trust in them is merely childish. In fact, few people do put their whole trust in such feelings; they are guided at least unconsciously by many other considerations.

If, however, one seeks a rule of thumb by which to measure the desirability of a partnership, the Primary

Sex Complex makes a good standard. Are all the five elements of this present in due proportion in the relationship? If so, go ahead. If one of them is absent, be careful. If several of them are lacking, stop—no matter how dizzying may be the sensations generated.

The difficulty with many marriages is that, instead of a solid foundation in the Primary Sex Complex, they have only part of a foundation. Many a marriage is based merely on the biological mating impulse. Important as that is, it is only one fifth of a foundation; and a marriage cannot be sustained long on one fifth of a foundation, any more than a bridge across the Mississippi River can be sustained on one fifth of a foundation.

Another marriage is based merely on the economic interest—"marrying a meal ticket." Comfortable as such as a procedure may be, it is not enough of a foundation for a permanent marriage!

Still others are based merely on interests in the children. Important as such interests are, they are not enough. One need but look around to see the disastrous results of basing a marriage merely on them. Such a mistake explains many of the divorces that occur after twenty or thirty years of marriage. They are becoming so common that few people can have escaped seeing them.

"So the Jenkins are getting a divorce!" one exclaims. "Why, I can hardly believe it. They have been married a quarter of a century. They have a son in Princeton, and their daughter was married last summer. I don't understand what's the matter!"

A very slight inspection of the Jenkins' home would show the matter. For years they have been supporting their marriage wholly on the children—on one fifth of a foundation. Everything else has gone, if it ever existed. The biological mating impulse is dead. The economic interests are not important. The sexually-colored comradeship has long since become a mockery. The non-sexually colored comradeship probably never did exist. For years all they have had in common is the children: they could think and talk and plan for Gladys and Dick. But now Gladys and Dick are gone, and they suddenly realize that they have nothing whatever in common—no foundation left. The walls of what was once a home collapse of their own weight.

All of the Elements Can Be Created or Nourished.

Yet all of these elements can be created or nourished. They do not come by magic; they are largely the product of intelligent cultivation.

The man who questions the depth and permanence of his own interest, therefore, need not wait for some intuitive inspiration or revelation but merely ask himself whether the five elements of the Primary Sex Complex are at least potentially present. Fortunately, all of them can be identified before marriage with the exception of parenthood: there is always a possibility that children, though greatly desired, will not appear; but in the "average normal" part of the population this contingency is too small to be a cause of anxiety, and, at the worst, there may be adoptions.[67]

If, on consideration of Mary Jane, Hugh decides that all the elements of the Primary Sex Complex are in sight, he can proceed without the slightest hesitation. If several of them are absent and he has no confident determination to create them, he will be well advised to look in a different direction, no matter how pleasing his emotions may be, no matter how fast his heart may beat when she whispers, "Honestly, Hughie, I just didn't dream that any man could be as wonderful as you are!"

If one wants to be still more specific, it is easy to find lists of rules or sets of questions that give material for an answer. The following are typical, but it would be possible to extend the list indefinitely:

1. Do I love her just as she is, with all her faults included?

2. Do I find greater happiness in her presence than anywhere else?

3. Do I like her family? or, if not, can I be sure that I will never have to associate with them—much less live with them and borrow money from them?

4. When not with her, am I continually wishing that I were?

5. Am I eager to defer to her—to give full weight to her wishes, opinions, and judgments?

6. Would I be not only willing, but glad, to spend

my whole life with her and sacrifice all activities not compatible with married life with her?

7. Do my plans keep unconsciously and insistently organizing themselves around her?

8. Is she the woman whom I would choose as the mother of my children?

9. Do I take pride in her and desire to show her off?

10. Do we have similar interests and cultural backgrounds? or, if not, is there reason to believe that we can and will develop such things in common?

11. Am I eager to share as many of my experiences as possible with her?

12. Are we both open to some improvement and adaptation to each other's tastes?

13. When we are together, do we find a great deal to talk about?

14. Does her presence or the thought of her stir my intellectual and emotional life into keen activity?

15. Am I eager for her success, for the fulfillment of her personality?

If such questions can be answered affirmatively, the prospects are good—or else the answerer is capable of extraordinary self-deception!

CHAPTER XI

MAN PROPOSES

CONTRARY to what is sometimes asserted, there are very few marriages indeed which have not followed some sort of formal proposal. Occasionally a couple say they merely "grew together"; that marriage was taken for granted without anything being said about it. A moment's thought will convince anyone that this cannot be literally true. One does not marry a girl without having mentioned the fact to her at some time or other, in some way or other, prior to the ceremony! This idea is, in fact, one of those rationalizations with which marriage is filled,—one of those after-thoughts that is soon accepted by husband and wife as the truth. Just as they force themselves, in time, to believe that they knew at first sight that they were made for each other, so they finally come to think that they never had a real proposal.

There is always a reason for a rationalization. Why do husband and wife affirm to themselves that there was no proposal, to the extent that they finally come to believe this? One who has studied the facts will have no doubt about the commonest explanation. The average proposal is so inept and inartistic that both are ashamed of it and want to live it down! The man wonders why he did not act more like a hero; the girl accepts it (if she does) because she wants the man and figures that she cannot afford to be too finicky. Sometimes she rejects him in order to make him try over again under more favorable auspices. Sometimes she is disappointed even then!

Many girls have had, in self-defense, to develop a sour grapes or sweet lemons compensation: to pretend that they would not want a poetic proposal. Any man who takes such allegations seriously is either a poor judge of feminine nature, or else is dealing with a rare and abnormal specimen of the female sex.

It is true that almost any kind of proposal may be a prelude to a successful marriage. Adele, a nurse, invited Zachary to a party at a hospital; Zach sat down in a dish of ice cream which had been placed in a chair, and Adele had to administer first aid. She did it so tactfully and successfully that he decided she was just the girl for him. His proposal on the spot was accepted, and they lived happily ever after.

It is equally true that a wholesome and satisfactory meal might follow a first course which was repellent. But why not let the whole thing be in harmony? Why should not the proposal be a keynote to the marriage? Why should it not show the same qualities of forethought, consideration, good taste, and devotion that will be required throughout the rest of life?

Emma had already been a two-time loser when she went to Montana to teach. In San Francisco one man had proposed to her while they were rushing for the entrance of a ferryboat. After she dropped him she began to go with a man who was a contractor and builder in a small way. One evening he took her out for a drive and stopped in front of a bungalow he had just finished. "That's where you and I are going to live and raise our family," he assured her bluntly. But he was mistaken. When she settled in Montana, a cowboy offered to teach her to ride, and they became well acquainted. Finally he took her to what she says is the most beautiful and romantic spot in the state; and as the full moon rose over the black buttes, he proposed to her. P.S.—He got the girl.

Many men are apparently so immature that they are incapable of making and carrying out any plan for a proposal. They have to depend on the spur of the moment; and sometimes it is a strange spur! For instance:

Alphonse, who was only nineteen, took a high school girl for a ride on a roller coaster. It was one of the scary kind, and both became so scared that he proposed and she accepted. Later the engagement was broken.

At a picnic, Stephen enjoyed the gooseberry pie which Dolores had made. He took her aside. "That pie was simply wonderful, Dolores!" he exclaimed ecstatically. "Will you marry me?" She wouldn't.

Florence was a city girl, unused to the ways of the wild. When she was hiking on a mountain trail with Claude and they almost stepped on a rattlesnake in the path, she became hysterical. He tried to comfort her, assured her that he would take care of her now and for-

ever, and asked her to marry him. She was too confused even to answer; but when she recalled it later,
the romance had worn off and there was no need of an
answer.

I know a number of cases in which the man got his
start by watching a love scene in the movies; he turns
to the girl at his side and inquires, "How about you and
me?"

Samuel's inspiration arrived when he heard that a
school near his ranch was vacant. He wrote to a teacher
with whom he was slightly acquainted and suggested
that she apply for it. "If you get it, you and I could
marry," he assured her.

If mankind is to improve on this technique, three
factors must be taken into account: timing, place,
manner.

The Timing of Proposals.

1. *The time to propose is when you have found the
right girl,* and when you are sure that she is not only
ready but eager to have you ask her. If you propose
sooner, you may be turned down; if you delay, you
may either lose her or put her into the embarrassing
position of having to propose to you.

In many previous chapters I have discussed the ways
in which you can know that you have found the right
girl. Here it is merely necessary to say that many a
man proposes when he does not know that he has found
the right girl. I could cite a dozen cases in which a

man proposed to a girl who was already engaged; several in which he proposed to a girl already married—in every case without having any idea of her status, of course. Why should even a fool propose to a girl about whom he knew so little? Proposals at a first meeting are in much the same classification. If a girl is worth having, she is not likely to accept a proposal from a man whom she has never seen before. If she is not worth having, the man is a fool to propose to her. Not even the divorce records give a more vivid picture of the infantile attitude of many men toward marriage than do the proposal records!

Premature proposal, far from convincing the girl—as you perhaps desire—that you are overwhelmingly smitten with her charms, may lead her to think that you do not value her for what she is (which you can not possibly know) but merely for what you can get out of her. A school nurse went to call at the home of a child whose father appeared (to her!) to be about eighty years old. After a few minutes talk about the welfare of the boy, he asked the nurse to marry him. In most of the cases of proposal at first sight, the man is either refused or told to "come later." He may have succeeded in his desire to make a strong impression on the girl, but is quite likely to repel her, especially if she feels conscious of family position, wealth, or some other extraneous attraction.

On the other hand, the man who delays may lose the girl altogether. She cannot wait indefinitely for him to make up his mind—or show that he has made it up.

Her best years are getting away from her too rapidly. Girls are continually facing this situation; are asking whether, if they have been "going steady" with a boy for some time, they ought to turn down invitations from other boys. They *think* that Louis is "in earnest", but he has never said so. Of course, in such circumstances the girl can only be told that she must take nothing for granted and should accept any other invitations that are interesting. If you are Louis, you may suddenly find that a rival has taken your girl away from you—and serve you right! After all, girls cannot afford to waste their time on some fellow who has not the courage of his convictions; they waste a great deal too much of their time that way now.

Recently I looked over a batch of papers written by junior college girls, who were asked among other things to state whether they were married, single, or engaged. Three of them said they were engaged; four said "Practically engaged"; and another wrote, "Am not married, but will become engaged soon." No law prohibits a young woman from hoping; and, after all, these were very young women. But if they do not know now, they will soon find out that a girl can not marry Hope.

It would be easy to cite "horrible examples" of men who have been wasting some girl's time for years in this manner. You, too, know unhappy illustrations from your own circle of acquaintances. Leonore and Harlow had been going together for several years; finally he went off on a long business trip. She thought he did not care for her, and married another man, in desperation. The shock of losing her was a heavy one to Harlow; while Leonore's attachment to Harlow has seriously handicapped the success of her marriage to Stuart. Why was not Harlow enough of a man to tell her how he felt about her, and not leave her to guesswork and fear?

If a man ought to propose but will not, what can a poor girl do? Either drop him, or else take the bit in her own teeth. Some girls are much too ready to propose, and of course gain nothing by it. In many instances they are dealing with men either considerably older or considerably younger than themselves, and feel that this age disparity makes it desirable for them to take more initiative than they otherwise would. The whole story of proposals by women has never been told, and perhaps never will be; but such evidence as exists (I myself have studied 150 cases) points very strongly to the fact that, however artistic they may be in other ways, women do not always do an artistic job of proposing. Carlos was packing up to leave his rooming house when his landlady came in, threw her arms around him, and sobbed, "I can't bear to lose you. Won't you please take me along with you?" Stella's escort had got drunk at the country club. She put him in a car, drove him home, got him up to his apartment, and then proposed to him. When he sobered up, he broke the engagement! Even in more normal surroundings, a woman's proposal almost invariably betrays the fact that she has taken a task which she did not want and does not like, but that she is going to put her pride in her pocket and make the best of a bad job. On the other hand, I suppose few men ever felt really flattered to have a woman propose to them.

Many of these woman-proposed marriages turn out successfully; but, as I remarked above, they are often a little out of the ordinary in some way. In most instances, neither the man nor his wife feels proud of the fact that she proposed. The answer is: If you want to marry her, don't wait for *her* to tell *you* so.

The Place of Proposals.

2. *If men often show little sense of timing, they often show even less sense of the fitness of things, in selecting a place to ask the question.* I have tabulated nearly twelve hundred proposals by men in half a dozen groups; the curious reader may refer to Appendix V for the exact figures. It transpires that no one type of place is favored much more than another. The woman's home provides the setting for about one fifth of the proposals. Many women nowadays have either no home suitable for the purpose, or no privacy in their home; hence four fifths of the proposals are staged elsewhere.

Since the automobile does provide a certain amount of privacy, it has largely supplanted the home for purposes of courtship; and the latest word in modernity is furnished by one of my clients who proposed in an airplane, of which he was pilot and his girl the passenger. The combination of privacy and propinquity which the parked car furnishes is evidently found to be as satisfactory as any other possibility that is generally available.

Acquaintances while traveling, or at resorts or vacation places, are famous for betrothals. They usually allow certain opportunities for privacy and at the same time make it possible for the partners to be together a great deal of the time. Even here, many men take little advantage of favorable opportunities, but apparently wait for the most unfavorable ones: Antoine proposed in a swimming pool, Christopher at a soda fountain, Samson on the platform of a railway station, Eugene in a cemetery.

The numbers involved in my table are not large enough to permit statistically incontrovertible comparisons; but on the face of the returns a proposal by letter brings a higher percentage of marriages than any other form. There is not much romance in it; but if a man proposes in this way he is pretty sure to be in earnest—he has not been caught unawares by propinquity. He has thought it over fully; and the recipient has time to do the same—she is not taken by surprise (yes, occasionally a girl *is* taken by surprise by a proposal), and forced to accept or reject on the spur of the moment. In spite of this favorable percentage, "direct by mail" methods are not to be recommended.

Another group is made up of proposals at some social affair—party, dance, theater, for instance. These have in common a pleasant and emotionally stimulating atmosphere, the girl usually appears at her best in dress and make-up; on the other hand the lack of privacy is a handicap, although some men are too obtuse to admit it to themselves. Randolph was on a bob-sled party and engaged in the traditional male vocation described as "keeping her warm." "Won't you let me always keep you warm?" he pleaded loudly in her ear. He was too elated to care who overheard him; but the girl, as is usual in such cases, was more sensitive to public opinion. Much embarrassed, she whispered to him to wait until they were alone and could talk it over—then accepted.

The last group (barring a few miscellaneous) is made up of proposals in public—on the street, in restaurants, public parks, on the campus, and in similar localities where there is neither privacy nor a romantic setting of any kind, in most instances. The large size of this group testifies to the difficulty which young people in cities find in getting privacy; still more, I think, does it testify to the lack of taste on the part of young men. "Window shopping proposals" are common. He and she are looking at the display of a furniture store, for instance, when he inquires, "How's about you and me fixing up a little love nest, huh?" Or they are before a jeweler's and he suggests, "Let's go in right now and get yours." More practical, Toby and Eunice were looking in the window of a shop selling electrical goods. A toaster was in the center of the exhibit, and Toby suddenly exclaimed, "How'd you like to toast my bread for me in the mornings, *permanently?*" Eunice accepted; but I am sure her heart sank.

I am citing exceptional cases, of course; yet the record shows all too clearly that the average man, no matter how long he has contemplated proposing, is likely to take the final plunge at a time and in a way that he himself does not anticipate. Once in a while there is a good explanation. Austin took Patricia out canoeing, and they tipped over. There was nobody else in sight; they clung to the canoe with every prospect of drowning. "If we live, will you marry me?" Austin ventured at length. With death staring her in the face, perhaps any other prospect looked good by contrast; at any rate she assented, they were rescued, and are still prospering as man and wife.

But in most cases it is evident that some extremely trivial circumstance was enough to precipitate the question at a really inopportune time. Constantine was a young physician who had been going for some months with one of the nurses in the hospital. Calling one evening at the Nurses' Home, without a date, he found she was preparing to go out with another man. He became childishly indignant; she equally so. "Say, mister, you haven't got any strings on me," she snapped at him. "Then I'll put some on you right now," he retorted angrily. "Will you be my wife?" "Well, sir," she related afterward, "it was just like having a bucket of cold water thrown over me"; but she accepted—'phoned the other man that she would have to break her date with him. Constantine had his way, and their family life has been a very happy one.

But marriage is too important to be left to chance,

even though this chance does involve the working out of deep-seated emotional trends.

The Manner of Proposals.

3. *Finally, there is the manner of proposing,* which is all too graphically illustrated in some of the cases that I have been citing. It is often crude and discouraging; though perhaps personal crudities are no worse than a proposal through a third party—the famous case of John Alden. I have several times been asked to act as intermediary in such a mission—so far in vain. I know of several cases in which a man got either his mother or the girl's mother to propose for him. The girl who agrees to marry such a man is indeed an optimist.

Even if he acts on his own behalf, the man may do so in an insulting way. Mrs. J. took her son along when she went to call on Mrs. K. The latter had a daughter a few years older than Junior; and, as the mothers talked together, the respective son and daughter sat and listened. The conversation ran to marriages between old and prominent families in the community. Junior leaned over and said to the young woman, "I think it would make our folks very happy if we did that." She at least affected not to understand him; and when they passed into the hall he drew near and whispered in a hurt tone, "Didn't you understand that I was asking you to marry me?"

Sometimes the occasion is so unromantic that it "goes

by contraries." Art, for instance, was chef at a small restaurant in which Mamie was a waitress. One day they had a terrible quarrel over a steak that went wrong; they blackguarded each other until everyone in the kitchen stopped work to take in the show. Finally Art exploded: "Look here, it's no use for us to try to work in the same place. Suppose you get out, and marry me instead." She did, and their marriage has been a distinct success.

Even more public was Homer's proposal. He was a vaudeville actor, and Hazel played in the orchestra. An important part of Homer's act consisted of repartee with members of the orchestra, and Hazel proved to have a particular talent for it. On the last day of his appearance, as part of the performance he leaned over the footlights and shouted, "By the way, sister, will you marry me?" "Certainly; name the day," Hazel shot back, while the audience roared its approval of the comedy. After the show he came down and said, "Of course I really meant that." "So did I," was her reply.

But an occasional spectacular proposal cannot offset the great bulk of dull, prosaic, uninspired, childish, inadvertent, and inappropriate proposals. Even if they are accepted and followed by a happy marriage, they have not been worthy of it. If marriage is to be taken seriously, should not proposal be taken more seriously? If successful marriage is an art that can be studied, why not begin with proposals?

How Many Proposals Does the
Average Girl Ever Receive?

That man is a constant practitioner, whether or not
he achieves art, may be assumed without statistical
evidence. Proposals have had too little study, and in
any event it is hard to be sure that informants will
tell the whole truth. But I have collected data on 208
women, through their close friends and relatives. Only
eleven of the group claimed never to have had a proposal, and most of these were young with opportunities
presumably still ahead of them. The two in this no-
proposal group who were over forty presumably represented careerists or unmarriageable women. It is very
possible that women who had never had a proposal
would be most likely to evade answering. If more ex-
tensive investigations bear out the findings of this first
small inquiry, it would appear (as is indeed popularly
supposed) that a few women never receive a single
proposal, but that the great bulk of the female population has had some offers of marriage, even though all
the offers may have been unacceptable.

In this group the average number of proposals per
woman was two and five-tenths; but if one takes the
maxima, it is fair to say that the average woman of the
type represented in this investigation will probably receive three proposals in the course of her lifetime. Seven
of the women claimed seven or more each; the largest
number, fourteen, being claimed by a very attractive
woman now about fifty years of age.

The age of the woman questioned was taken either at the time of inquiry, if she was still unmarried, or as of the time of marriage, if she was a married woman; the supposition being that she would receive no further proposals after she became a wife! Distributed by age, the number of proposals was as follows:

AGE	NUMBER OF WOMEN	AVERAGE NUMBER OF PROPOSALS
18 and under..............	33	1.5
19-20	54	2.3
21-22	37	2.7
23-24	19	2.9
25-26	19	2.8
27-28	15	2.9
29-30	8	4.7
over 30	23	2.9
All	208	2.5

Without laying much stress on the small numbers involved in this isolated study, one would infer that a girl gets most of her proposals in the early twenties.

Chapter XII

THE BETROTHAL PERIOD

Yes, you are telling your friends, "We're engaged."

What does that mean? What is the purpose of betrothal?

The Purpose of Betrothal Among
Civilized Peoples.

It is a purely human institution, not found among other mammals, where mating follows immediately after courtship and acceptance. It exists among some tribes of low culture, but only in rudimentary form. As people become more civilized, a formal period of betrothal comes to be more and more prominent in their customs. Sometimes it becomes almost as binding as marriage itself. Presumably it would not have developed in this way unless it had some useful functions.[80] Among these are:

1. *It gives a chance to correct a mistake.* As marriage becomes more permanent, more complicated, more important, more valuable, it is more and more necessary that partners get the right start. Two young people have become engaged. As pointed out in the preceding chapter, this has sometimes happened unex-

pectedly and with little previous acquaintance. Even those who have known each other for years may decide, on closer acquaintance, that they are not adapted to each other; possibly not adapted to marriage at all. What is to be done in such a case? Obviously it is desirable that they be able to change their minds before any binding commitments have been made. They can "break off the engagement."

It would not be correct to think, as a few people seem to, that engagements are made merely to be broken! But at least engagements ought to be breakable; and when they are considered to be as binding as marriage, as is the case in a few groups, they lose this value. If a mistake has been made, it is highly desirable that it be rectified, with as little damage as possible, by breaking the engagement, rather than with as great damage as possible, by a divorce some years later.

That the institution does work effectively in this way is evidenced by the number of persons who have been engaged several times before marriage.

I have collected data on 141 men and 194 women in the educated part of the population. All were married at the time they were questioned. It transpired that most of them (55 per cent of the men and 77 per cent of the women) had had at least one previous engagement.

In this particular inquiry, there was little evidence of many frivolous engagements. Perhaps the informants did not tell the whole truth; or perhaps in this part of the population people do tend to take engage-

ments seriously. Of those who had been engaged prior
to the betrothal that resulted in marriage, few had been
engaged more than once or twice. One man reported
four previous engagements; three women matched him
with four engagements apiece; while one woman
claimed seven, and another eight.

The number of engagements was compared with the
age at marriage on the assumption that one who married at thirty would have had time for more engagements, and therefore might have had more, than one
who married at twenty. This turned out to be true
of men, but not of women. The figures for the men
were as follows:

Age at Marriage	No. of Men	No. of Engagements	Engagements per Man
Under 25	63	29	.46
25-29	47	45	1.0
30 and over	31	40	1.3

In each case, the engagement which led to the marriage
is not counted.

In the case of the thirty-six women who married under the age of twenty, there had been only seventy-
eight hundredths of a prior engagement each. But in
the succeeding age groups, the average was almost exactly one prior engagement per woman.

Much larger numbers are needed to answer all possible questions, but these figures agree with what one
might expect. It would appear that men do have more
chances to marry, as represented by the slight increase
in betrothals with advancing age. With women, whose

marriageable years are so few, it is not a question of age but of personality and inherent marriageability, including attractiveness, fickleness, and all other characteristics. One woman will attain as many engagements in a couple of years as will another in a couple of decades, the number in any case not being large.

Sometimes an Engagement
Should be Broken.

In most of the relationships between the sexes, tradition and custom expect the man to take the initiative. In breaking off an engagement, however, the initiative is largely in the hands of the woman, for the reasons that I pointed out in Chapter V. This does not mean that a man should not change his mind, when experience compels. Presumably, however, he may have to make a little more effort to persuade his fiancée that it is for the good of all concerned that the engagement be broken, so that she will acquiesce at least formally, no matter how unwillingly. No man owes it to any girl to marry her against his will, unless he has assumed obligations that do not leave him a free agent. The time for him to stop and think is before he assumes any obligations. But if it is merely a case of an ordinary betrothal, and he is now sincerely convinced that the marriage would be a misfortune, he should recognize that one of the purposes of the betrothal period is to prevent such misfortunes by giving either participant a chance to turn back before the bridge is burned. In the long run, it is not to the interest of any girl to be married to a man who wedded her against his will and continually reminds himself of that fact— probably is ungallant enough continually to remind *her* of that fact, as well!

2. *The betrothal period is also an apprenticeship in mutual accomodation*, so that the adjustment of two hearts to beat as one, even when they started with widely different rates of pulsation, does not have to be entirely carried out after marriage.

Francis and Frances were born and brought up in different parts of the country. They are of different ancestry, different education, and different church affiliations. They have learned to work differently, play differently, eat differently, drink differently, talk differently, act differently, and think differently. The differences are slight in a way, yet they total up to a large stock. They will make life more interesting for the two, provided that Francis and Frances take them that way. But it will be safer to take them as a gradual inoculation, which will prevent a serious outbreak later on, just as a gradual inoculation with typhoid will prevent a serious attack.

Now is the time for Francis and Frances to study each other—and to study themselves. He will find that she is not always punctual.[19] This is a good time for him to learn how to deal with that peculiarity. When they are going out, will he put on his hat ostentatiously while she is still dressing; then announce in a tone of injured innocence that he will go out and sit in the automobile; and in a few minutes more begin to honk the horn? Or will he make allowances for the many things she must do other than putting on *her* hat, before she leaves the house? Will he be annoyed by her dislike of drafts, because he is a fresh air fiend? Will he be infuriated because, when she comes back from a shopping trip, she has no idea what she has spent? Will he be even more infuriated because, when she has spent the whole day shopping, she comes home without having spent anything? Will he take the position that whatever he himself does must be immune from criticism?

Three years ago they were complete strangers. Three months from now they will be living together in the greatest intimacy possible for two human beings. A thousand differences will have to be adjusted. If two perfect strangers were pitched instantaneously into the condition of perfect intimacy, they would have to make these thousand adjustments all at once. If they can make them, instead, at the average rate of one a day over several years, it will be an easier task! The betrothal period is naturally used, and should be consciously and consistently used, to build up a habit of give-and-take, of sharing, of tolerance for difference of opinion, of acceptance of the partner "as is" rather than as one to be rebuilt to new specifications as quickly as possible.

3. *The betrothal period likewise enables the partners to mature emotionally.* It stimulates their biological and

psychological development; it brings them closer and closer together until the final and perfect union.

Represented in a diagram, too many marriages would show the partners moving along more or less on a level, until there came a sudden and violent break in the line on the wedding night, the continuation being on an entirely different plane. Such an abrupt transition is undesirable, sometimes harmful. The ideal would be a smooth curve steadily ascending, with a scarcely perceptible alteration after the wedding ceremony. In other words, the lovers, starting from the day of betrothal (which itself is merely a point in a line leading from their first meeting) should approach each other gradually, mounting steadily to higher elevations, until they step into the complete intimacy of lifelong union and continue to ascend, as one, to greater and greater heights of happiness.

This requires good management. Many marriages fail because they have fallen too far off the line on one side or the other.

Most young people start off on this line with a large store of inhibitions surrounding the realities of love. These have played a useful part; one who lacks them is not likely to go far.[104] But they may become a defect which locks the wheels of the car instead of being merely a brake to control its speed. Girls probably suffer in this way more than do boys; but both sexes have too often grown up with fears and fixations, with emotional tie-ups that prevent normal and independent development. Men and women alike, in some instances, enter the betrothal period with such starved, warped, atrophied, or rudimentary emotional equipment that they are far from ready for marriage; and a serious purpose of the betrothal period must be to bring them nearer to each other, to build up mutual understanding and confidence, to break down one by one the barriers that separate the two sexes, until by the wedding day they will be prepared each to surrender wholly to the other, without shock, without any feeling except that of the naturalness and inevitableness of the whole proceeding.

Unsatisfactory Forms of "College Engagements."

While the usefulness of the betrothal period, in promoting better sexual selection, is destroyed by making it too binding, the other extreme of taking it too lightly and frivolously is even more prejudicial to success in marriage. Trivial betrothals are usually entered into, either from a childish desire to gain a feeling of power, or from the need for a feeling of security, or else as a cover for intimacies that would not otherwise be acceptable.

"College engagements" sometimes include all three of these factors. They reflect some of the unwholesome characteristics of much social life in certain large co-educational colleges and universities. For the college man, social life is, for the most part, a means to recreation. For the college woman social life is in many in-

stances largely an end in itself: her prestige, social repute, membership in organizations, may depend not
merely on her having an escort for every affair, but on
her having a "socially desirable" escort to every affair.
She therefore feels herself forced—in fact may be forced
by her sorority sisters or other associates—to sacrifice
many other things to the maintenance of her "social
position."

As a freshman, Irene enters college with the advantage of novelty in addition to whatever attributes she
may have that are important for the purpose—beauty,
vivacity, social connections, family background. The
"right kind" of men take her up, and she sacrifices
everything to keep in the current. But in a couple of
years two new groups of freshmen girls have appeared
with the same advantages that Irene had at the start
of her college career. The men, who are socially and
biologically less mature than she is, anyway, are at-
tracted to the newcomers and prepared to drop her.
She will thereupon be left without escorts or else will
have to take those whom she formerly considered
second- or third-raters; and that, she feels, is equivalent
to social suicide.

How can Irene hold her ground when it is so slippery?
The easiest way is to become engaged, in her sophomore
or junior year, to one of the more desirable men; thereafter he cannot stray away toward attractive new freshmen girls; she can hold him by virtue of the fact that
they are betrothed. Being more mature and cleverer
than the boys in her class with whom she is going, she

"takes a pin", she becomes engaged, at least in an implicit and informal way, to one of them. She may overexploit sex-appeal to get him, or she may use this as a means to hold him. The engagement may fall of its own weight after they graduate, or even before; but for the time being it has served its purpose in enabling her to "go steady."

Of course not all college engagements are of this sort; but anyone familiar with the snobbish and selfish social life that exists in certain circles of certain universities will be acquainted with this type. Many successful marriages doubtless result; but the college man should be sure, if he enters a betrothal before graduation, that it is related to his own future and not merely a convenient way for some desperate young woman to assure herself a steady supply of tickets to the games and a full program at the "proms." In so far as such a betrothal is intended merely to throw a blanket of pseudo-respectability over sexual intercourse, its effects will be discussed forthwith.

Premarital Intercourse Threatens the Success of the Marriage.

It is occasionally alleged that premarital sexual experimentation has increased greatly among young people during the last generation. Of course it is impossible to get any satisfactory evidence on such a question; but there is certainly no evidence to uphold the contention. All the evidence [34] suggests that a majority of young people in the educated part of the population (there are no studies worth mentioning at other levels) go into marriage without any previous experience of sexual intercourse. There is some indication,[108] however, that intercourse during the betrothal period is commoner than it used to be; and there is also some evidence of the unfavorable consequences.

Of course it is possible that only the unfavorable cases come to light. However, so many unfavorable cases do come to light, and the disadvantages are so obvious, that they should be taken into account.

In the first place, an unexpected pregnancy often occurs. You have been telling your friends that you are to be married next June. Suddenly you inform them that you are to be married tomorrow—or that you were married yesterday. Everyone understands. It is not a dignified way to begin marriage, to say the least.

In the second place, one of the partners often carries over into marriage unconscious feelings of guilt, shame, disgust, or dissatisfaction, which are largely, perhaps wholly, unrecognized, but which create unexpected difficulties later on.

In the third place, the husband may use the fact of premarital intimacy as a ground for later suspicion of his wife. "She gave herself once to a man who was not her husband," he will assert; "how do I know that she won't do it again?" Even though this is merely a rationalization, or a projection to cover up his own infidelities, it is no help to the success of the marriage.

In the fourth place, it "takes the edge off" of marriage—to use a popular and significant expression. "Our engagement was a long one because of financial difficulties," Perry told me. "Sybil and I felt that we belonged to each other; that we were mated spiritually; and we had intercourse off and on for nearly a year before marriage. We didn't realize then, but we have realized since, how foolish we were. The need of secrecy and concealment, the need of separating just when we wanted to stay together, spoiled what should have been a perfect experience. The symphony of marriage is too fine to be started on such a keynote. Everything ought to be open and above board."

Finally, and in a surprisingly large number of cases, the husband later uses the fact of premarital intercourse as a weapon against his wife. Chauncey ends every quarrel with the same climax: "Torture me all you want to," he urges dramatically. "It's all my fault, I brought it on myself. When I married you, I knew I was making a mistake. When I walked up the church aisle, I felt as if I were walking to the gallows. I knew that I would suffer all the rest of my life for marrying you, but we had gone so far that I didn't have the courage to back out. I wish I had killed myself instead!" Such a chivalrous way of conducting a debate with a wife is not calculated to promote successful marriage!

Some, through distrust of themselves, cannot attain the deepening and enrichment of experience that successful marriage alone affords. It is these who err on the opposite side. They have so cheapened the sexual partnership by putting it on an infantile level of self-indulgence, that they are unable thereafter to transform it into an adult relationship.[104] As is well known, all studies show that the happiest marriages are between persons neither of whom has had any previous sexual experience. Why, again, is previous sexual experience undesirable? Sometimes because the kind of person who had it was undesirable—an immature, self-centered, self-seeking person who cannot make a success of any real adult enterprise because he never can be an adult.

It is a mistake, then, to turn the betrothal period into a common-law marriage, just as it is a mistake to look on it as a mere lark. Successful marriage will be promoted by recognizing its purpose and using it wisely for that purpose.

How Soon To Marry?

A study [101] of marriages that were not preceded by any formal betrothal suggests one answer. In a group of 436 educated marriages taken from the population at large, only 5 per cent reported no formal period of betrothal before marriage. Among unhappily married clients of the Institute of Family Relations, 40 per cent reported no betrothal.

The couples who reported no betrothal had known each other almost as long as the rest (an average of twenty months). Why, after this acquaintance, did they marry on impulse, on the spur of the moment? Many of them were perhaps unstable persons, unable to plan their own futures intelligently or to carry out plans if they made them. A formal period of betrothal might have saved them a good deal of difficulty.

Length of acquaintance before betrothal does not tell the whole story because a couple might have met in childhood but have seen little or nothing of each other until brought together ten years later. Suppose they married after a six weeks' courtship: they would report that they had been acquainted for ten years; but the period of effective acquaintance, so to speak, would be put more correctly at six weeks. Failure to make this distinction probably accounts for some confusion in the findings of several studies of the subject. In general, however, other investigators confirm our finding that those who marry happily have known each other longer, have been going together longer, and have a longer engagement than those whose marriages turn out badly.

This does not deny that some marriages on very short acquaintance do turn out successfully. If people see a good deal of each other, a year ought to be enough for them to decide whether they want to plan for marriage. Women are perhaps able to make up their minds, or "size up their men," more rapidly than are their partners.[108]

It might be supposed that a long acquaintance would be followed by a correspondingly shorter engagement. The reverse is the case: those who have known each other longest tend also to have longer engagements than the average.[101]

The average engagement is about a year in length—

somewhat longer in the professional classes, shorter in the skilled and unskilled labor groups. Very long engagements often fall of their own weight and therefore do not get into the statistics. A prolonged engagement sometimes indicates either lack of purpose on the part of one partner, or else a lack of genuine interest. Long engagements that do survive often lead to successful marriages, because they represent people who had enough persistence and determination to pursue their plans steadily; but they are objectionable because of the emotional strain, if the couple are together a great deal.

Chapter XIII

MUST YOU DIG UP THE PAST?

How much of The Past should you tell the woman you expect to marry?

It is sometimes argued that partners should have no secrets from each other. If anything less than "the truth, the whole truth, and nothing but the truth" is told, the marriage is not on that foundation of complete trust and mutual confidence that is desirable. One must tell all.

Opinions differ greatly, however. I asked a group of forty-five graduate students to write out their views on this point. In substance nine said, "Tell all"; thirty advised, "Use discretion"; six urged, "Tell nothing".

With all these differences of opinion, many people have strong convictions to support their own views. In practice, each must answer the question for himself. I shall merely state my own opinion without wanting to force it on anyone else. I agree with the intermediate group above mentioned who considered that one should use some judgment in what he tells.

Obviously, no man can possibly "tell all" in the literal meaning of the words. Even if he took the floor to filibuster for a year without stopping, he would make only a beginning on the entire mass of experience, almost all of it trivial or routine, that represented a lifetime. You are evidently going to make not only a selection, but a narrow and stringent selection, of some kind for the purpose of narration. In actual practice, how are you going to decide what to tell? On what basis are you going to select certain things from this great mass, to pass on? Are you, merely to make yourself feel important, going to dramatize a few sensational exploits, under pretense that you feel obliged to "confess"? A good deal of the confession before marriage appears to me to be motivated largely by a childish desire to show off; though certainly the narrator who is dragging out a lot of commonplace unpleasantnesses to force on his partner's attention does not recognize, and would not admit to himself, that exhibitionism was his real motive.

This is merely infantile, but another motive is contemptible; namely, the effort to draw the girl out. Herman was one of the petty, tyrannical, childishly possessive persons whose overweening curiosity made him a nuisance to all his friends and relatives. He became engaged to a girl whom he met while traveling. He knew little about her background, but he could not endure to let her live her own life; she must live only through him. He worked up to the subject gradually, with the usual effusive protestations that "Nothing in the world could ever make any difference to our love." At last he set the stage, with emotional assurances to her that "Lovers like us could not conceal anything from each other," and gave her a long story, partly imaginary, of his Don Juan career. Then he sat back expectantly for her to walk into the trap. Poor Dorothea felt that she ought to show equal faith in him, especially since he virtually demanded it; so she confessed to a silly schoolgirl escapade. Almost at once she noted a change in his manner; and within a few weeks he had not only dropped her abruptly but had passed the word to some of their mutual acquaintances, with a great affectation of mystery, that it almost killed him to give her up but that he had learned some things which changed the situation.

Occasionally, on the other hand, a man tries to unburden himself because of a deep inferiority complex—though this is commoner among women.

Again, the greatly increased intimacy (particularly during the honeymoon) sometimes leads to a sharing of experience that was not intended.

Finally, many persons—probably most of them—are actuated by a deeply honest unwillingness to sail under false colors, to be taken for anything except what they really are.

In this event, a man is more concerned about telling the unpleasant things than the favorable ones. Such a selection is unbalanced. Looking at the question more broadly, and following the popular idea that it is the discreditable facts which you want to tell, it seems to me that these facts fall into three groups.

Tell Her, If It's Really
Important.

1. *Some of these things may be of vital importance to your wife's future.* In that case, be honest, no matter how much it hurts. If you have a serious inheritable defect in your family; if you have at some time been committed as insane; if you know of some impediment which might prevent you from having children or living in a normal sexual partnership; if anything of this order of seriousness is involved, tell her frankly and fully, just as quickly as you can, and stand by the consequences no matter how painful. Do not put any pressure on her; leave her entirely free to consult what she believes to be her own interests, rather than make her feel that this is a time when she must show her loyalty to you.

2. *On the other hand, there may be unpleasant things which are really of no consequence to her,* but which she is going to find out sooner or later anyhow. If you do not tell her, someone else will. It is merely a matter of calculating expediency to do the telling yourself. It may be uncomfortable, but you will feel more uncomfortable if she hears it from someone else.

When Belle married Martin, it was against her parents' wishes. They told her he would never amount to anything; but he told her they were mistaken, and she believed him. A year later, one of Martin's business rivals found that Martin had served a term in the penitentiary. He got Martin's record and a copy of his photograph from the rogue's gallery and turned them over to Belle's father. The latter handed them to Martin's employer, who promptly fired the boy without giving any reason. The difficulties that resulted have not yet been straightened out, four years later. Martin should have known that such a record, like the fact of illegitimate birth,[56] or of adoption, or of expulsion from college, or of a previous marriage, is almost certain to come to light.

If you are going to be called upon to do a lot of explaining, it is much better to do it in your own way, at your own convenience, than to be put on the defensive later. That is perhaps not a very high ethical point of view, but it is certainly "enlightened self-interest."

3. *Most of the questions involved are much less dramatic,* much less important. Many of them are of importance to no one except yourself. Many things that you might tell could not be of any conceivable advantage to your wife, and might be a detriment. In such matters, I personally do not see why a man cannot mind his own business. It would be a misfortune if no one could ever live down any mistake he might have made; if every peccadillo were tied around his neck forever, like the dead albatross to the Ancient Mariner, as a source of offense to every stranger who passed by on the leeward side. If your conscience punishes you, why should you force the innocent to suffer with the guilty by trying to punish your wife?

*Don't Base Your Confessions on
Your Own Ignorance.*

It must be remembered that some of your confessions may originate in your own ignorance. A study [49] of 417 fraternity men in various middle western universities showed that they failed to answer correctly one third of the questions embodied in a simple outline of the facts of sex and reproduction that ought to have been easy for any junior high school boy. Certainly girls are no less ignorant. A mutual effort, both before and after marriage, to clear up ignorance is good education; but do not penalize your wife for your own previous failure to educate yourself.

Fritz, anxious to be honest with his fiancée, confessed to her that he had practiced masturbation. Various studies [17] show that from 60 per cent to 90 per cent or more of all young men have had some experience of masturbation; but his reading of quack literature had led him to believe that it was not merely a sin and a vice, but that it might even cause insanity. Surely anything that threatened their future happiness in that way was something his fiancée was entitled to know in advance. Gretchen was even more ignorant than he— too ignorant to realize that, according to various studies,[17] two-thirds of educated girls also have practised masturbation and that, in both sexes, it is regarded by physiologists as a relatively negligible matter. She felt that he was a marked man; and, for some years after their marriage (until both acquired a little elementary education), she was constantly on the lookout for the evidences of mental decay, constantly imagining that in some action of his she could detect the consequences of this sin. What if he should go insane? What would become of her and little Mildred? Indisputably, Fritz had done his wife an unpardonable wrong by foisting on her his own ignorance.

The fact is that young children show such a tendency to masturbate that many students have considered it a normal manifestation, on a par with the child's experiments in sticking his finger in his eye, or putting beans up his nostrils—all alarming to the young mother, but certainly not to be regarded as evidences of moral depravity.

As the child grows older, he normally outgrows this experimental period; in so far as any sexual feeling is involved, it is no longer turned so completely inward on himself, but is directed outward toward persons of the other sex. Boys who are habitual masturbators therefore represent, from a purely psychological point of view, a stage of arrested development; they are still in a childhood stage, from which they should have graduated.

With the young adult, masturbation may be on a different plane if it occurs only occasionally as a relief of an overstimulated sexual disposition. Even here, the normal safety valve is the nocturnal emission, and this is ordinarily sufficient to give relief; but if it is delayed past the point of comfort, and the man masturbates for relief, he need not think that he has damaged himself physically.

The chronic masturbator, who forms the habit of practicing this as a means of excitement, is of course on a different level. He is headed in the wrong direction: he is back in the infantile stage, and it may be hard for him to get away from it. Too many men are trying to maintain marriage on an infantile level of self-indulgence!

Any harmful effects of masturbation are therefore mental, not physical. One who has formed the habit should face it intelligently; not by some of the means ordinarily suggested, which merely focus attention on it and thereby intensify it; but by paying as little attention to it as possible and concentrating on a well-balanced and interesting life. It will rarely be difficult, in this way, to keep it within bounds.

Such scattered information as is available indicates that the number of young men who are promiscuous before marriage is very small. Of those who report that they have had any previous sexual intercourse, it is found [49] that in some instances this was a childhood experiment which could more properly be called "sex play"; and that in many of the other cases the experience was limited to a few attempts, perhaps only one, and often as a result of virtual seduction by an older woman,[59] perhaps a frustrated divorcee who could not find a partner of her own age. The whole episode was so unromantic and disaffecting that the man had no desire to repeat it, recognizing that what he had been offered was not an opportunity to be initiated into "the sex life," but merely to contribute, physically or financially, to the convenience of another person.

Most men fully understand that fragmentary episodes of this sort, associated with fear of detection, fear of pregnancy, fear of venereal disease, and the other usual accompaniments, have little in common with the genuine sharing of personalities that builds sex solidly into a life-pattern.

Psychologically, therefore, a large part of these premarital episodes represent no adult relationship, but a combination of infantile and adolescent deviations from the normal path of development toward happiness. The man who has thus jeopardized his own attainment of maturity should make it his first business to overcome any undesirable effects psychologically. If he has incurred any damage, his next responsibility is to see that he does not damage his wife in turn.

Both Partners Need Competent Counseling Before Marriage.

His fiancée, on the other hand, may have her own problems; not necessarily the same, but involving comparable decisions. He can only hope and expect that she will adopt the same policy he has followed, of complete honesty in essentials. She, too, runs the risk of encountering ignorance if she attempts to discuss her difficulties with him. She, too, will do better to discuss them, at least in the first instance, with some competent, impersonal, professional counselor.

Homosexuality is a case in point. So much sensational and pseudo-scientific attention has been given to it during the past few decades that it has become a matter of general discussion which, however, has by no means produced general enlightenment. By most persons it is regarded, quite correctly, as a serious perversion.

Suppose a young woman confesses to you that she was a homosexual during her college days. Probably neither one of you is in a position to evaluate this statement intelligently, and great harm may follow. The fact is that many girls drift into emotional relationships with others of their own sex during the adolescent period; that these frequently extend to the point of sexual stimulation; and that, technically speaking, they are homosexual relationships. A study [17] of a thousand educated married women showed that one in every seven had had such experiences, and that these episodes had no more bearing on the happiness of her subsequent marriage, or on her complete sexual normality in marriage, than does adolescent masturbation in a man. They are very different from genuine homosexual fixation, which involves a deep and usually permanent change of interest, apparently brought about as the result of the wrong kind of education.[110] If any young woman in whom you are interested feels called upon to enlighten you as to her past physical relationships with other girls, it is to be hoped that both you and she will have some educational preparation for understanding what she is talking about.

The individual's attitude toward sex, before marriage, also furnishes possibilities of confusion. I have already emphasized, above, that if a man is abnormal in this respect he should not allow any woman to marry him in ignorance. I now add, as emphatically as possible, that he should not allow himself to marry in ignorance either, but should work out the problem with some competent advisor, before he discusses it elsewhere.

Men [108] who, before marriage, have an attitude of disgust or aversion toward sex are less happy in marriage than those whose outlook is more normal and expressed in interest and pleasant anticipation. But those whose attitude is one of "eager and passionate longing" also are less happy than the average, in marriage. Intense preoccupation with the subject before marriage is not a normal outlook either, usually representing a somewhat neurotic tendency.*

Young men are sometimes advised that, during the adolescent years, they must expect to be the victims of an overwhelming sexual urge; that they have a continuous battle to fight with their "lower natures." I think

* These are, of course, the persons who seize most eagerly on opportunities to express themselves in questionnaires and other investigations not scientifically planned. When one sends out questionnaires and gets a reply from one in five, or one in ten, of the recipients, as often happens, there is good reason to suspect that those who reply are not a fair sample of the whole group, and that conclusions drawn from their replies may not be valid for the whole group. Many popular and journalistic investigations of the supposed opinions of young people are of little value for this reason.

it is the experience of most young men that this is non-sense. The man who marries at the usual age, and who before marriage has not deliberately subjected himself to overstimulation, rarely has to make any tremendous effort to resist this alleged imperious dominance of physiological urges. Everyone knows that these urges become strong after they have been expressed habitually, but that the formation of habit is a gradual process. Some of the difficulties of young men (and of young women, too) before marriage are certainly to be credited much more to wrong education than to nature. Usually a recreational program which emphasizes sex-releasing activities—that is, those in which both sexes participate but in which the group, not the individual partner, is the focus—will solve the problem. Those who deliber-ately choose sex-stimulating activities, in which the in-dividual partner is the focus, are merely looking for trouble. As I have pointed out repeatedly, it is likely to be the man (or woman) who is badly educated, lacks feelings of security and self-confidence, has an in-feriority complex, who is continually worried about sex; and it is not surprising that such persons are less happy than the average in marriage.[29]

While an attitude of disgust and aversion to sex, on the part of the man, is unfavorable to later good adjust-ment, such an attitude, as well as the much commoner attitude of indifference, on the part of women has little relationship to later good adjustment in marriage.[108]

Now if two persons are engaged in a game of com-petitive confession, before marriage, the man would not cite as one of his defects an eager and passionate longing for sexual intercourse; he would probably consider it a manly virtue. Yet it is one of the things that may handicap him. The woman, on the other hand, would probably consider a feeling of disgust or aversion for sex as a defect which she ought to admit; yet it may not handicap her later, in the slightest way. I am underlining these facts to call attention to the need of correct information and good judgment, before starting out to "tell all."

Whether you tell "all", tell nothing, or tell what you think is desirable, is something that you yourself must decide. Your decision on this point is part of your general preparation for marriage; it is one phase of the process which makes the period of betrothal a period of genuine education for successful marriage. If you have guided your life in the past in such a way as to keep it pointed toward successful marriage, you will probably find, as you review your past mistakes, that many of them give you some cause for chagrin, but few give you much cause for alarm. On the other hand, if you have gone off on a tangent, it is more important for you to take effective steps to solve any problems that you may thus have created for yourself, than it is for you to unload these problems, unsolved, on the head of your fiancée and think that in doing so you are particularly virtuous and, in some unascertainable way, proving that you are an ideal prospect as a husband.

CHAPTER XIV

HOW SOON CAN YOU AFFORD TO MARRY?

How much money do you need for marriage? The old answer, "Ten per cent more than you have," is a conservative estimate at best, but quite inadequate if you have none at all. Many young men have faced marriage with even less!

Obviously, it is desirable for a young couple to have an income on which they can live comfortably, but no one can possibly say how much this is. It depends on what they are accustomed to; what they hope to become accustomed to; the standard of living of their friends; whether they are living near their parents and have to move in somewhat the same social circles, or whether they are isolated and can adopt any standard necessary. Finally, it depends on their own managerial ability.

Young people looking forward to marriage naturally tend to see it in romantic pictures, based on art and imagination rather than on their own budget. When they are asked, in earlier years, what they think is the minimum amount on which two persons should marry, their ideas are often absurdly high in comparison with the possibilities.

In one college 285 boys and girls stated [32] the amounts they thought requisite for marriage. The average boy regarded $4,000 a year as adequate, with a nest egg of $3,500 as a starter. The average girl thought $4,500 was about right to maintain a reasonable standard of living, while there ought to be $4,000 in the bank before the wedding. Most of these students would not have that much wealth, even after twenty years in their professions or vocations!

That study was made in 1929. Ten years later I asked seven graduate students to write essays discussing the minimum amount on which an educated couple could marry, the assumption being that the husband's salary represented the only income—the wife did not work. The students in this seminar were married persons and documented their remarks by reference to their own experience. One named $80 a month, one $85; three mentioned $100, one $120; and the seventh voted for $150 a month as the minimum. On almost the same day, newspapers carried details of a study made of the teaching fellows and research assistants at one of the most famous American colleges. These men, all of whom have the Ph.D., are paid $75 a month; the inquirer was trying to find out how a married man in such a position could live on $75 a month. All the evidence showed that they did live. In most instances the wife helped out in some way. And, of course, children were hardly to be considered on that wage, with the standard of living that is expected of a college faculty.

The girl you want to marry thinks, in a vague way, that the man she marries should have $2,400 a year—or whatever it may be. You have not that much. Nevertheless, in a moment of enthusiasm she agrees to marry you. How are you going to pay the bills? Different men adopt different plans:

When the Wife Works After Her Marriage.

1. *The wife may keep her job after marriage,* or get one if she is not already working. This is the expedient most commonly adopted, and it involves a postponement of childbearing. Since no contraceptive is foolproof or, even under favorable conditions, is 100 per cent dependable, there is always the possibility of an unexpected pregnancy, which will change the "financial set-up." Often this does not turn out to be the disaster that was feared: the relatives help out, and it may eventually be a blessing in disguise. But at best it wrecks the financial plans on which the marriage was based.

"It certainly wrecked ours," Bessie told me. "Edgar and I wanted a family, but we agreed we would both have to work for some years. He hadn't even paid off his college debts. Then just a couple of months after the wedding I became pregnant. We were both panicky, but my mother was simply furious. She had wanted me to wait and not marry until Edgar was in better shape financially, and now she thought we'd come back and live with her. She insisted that I have an abortion. I told her I wouldn't start my married life with murder; that we'd go on relief if necessary, but we were going to see it through. After all, that was one of the reasons we had married. She wouldn't speak to me for two or three weeks, but she finally came around all right. I kept my job until just about a month before the baby was born. All our friends were simply swell. Edgar worked harder than ever before; when the baby came, his boss found out about it and gave him a fine raise. Sonny was born in June just as the schools were letting out, and a kid cousin of mine in high school, who had nothing to do in the vacation, practically moved in with us and helped me, so I didn't have to hire anyone; she got a great kick out of it and a liberal education in family relations, too. I suppose we had a lot of luck; but anyhow, we got by OK, and gee! we wouldn't trade Sonny for a million dollars!"

Sometimes the difficulty is reversed—the babies do not come soon enough for the good of the marriage. Joe and Carrie were getting $75 a month each. Their joint earnings of $150 did not seem to them to be a very large income. They lived up to it; and if either got a raise, they lived up to the raise. After five years they had not saved a cent. They began to think it was time for a baby if they were ever going to have one; but when they began to figure the cost, it did not make sense. They did not have enough to live on, as it was. If Carrie gave up her job for motherhood, their income would be cut in halves at the very moment that they would be needing more money instead of less! They could not see any answer, so they gave up the idea of children and have regretted it ever since.

There are still other difficulties. Sometimes the husband's self-esteem cannot face the fact that his wife must work to help support the establishment. He considers it a personal humiliation to him. This is a childish attitude in the circumstances, but is sometimes bolstered by his parents or her parents.

Worse still, sometimes his self-esteem goes by the board, as did that of Ellery, whose wife told the story: "With the very start of the depression, El lost his job. I had a life-certificate for teaching, and by a stroke of luck I heard that the school where I taught before marriage needed a teacher. The board was friendly to me and gave me my old job when I explained the circumstances. Anyhow, I was a good teacher, if I do say so. My mother took the children, while El began to hunt for another job. But there weren't many jobs to be had; and the bills were always paid promptly on the first of the month anyhow, because I was making more money than he had been getting. He was a skilled mechanic and didn't like to take a day-laborer's job even if he could have gotten one. I suppose you can't blame him much for that. But pretty soon I discovered that no job he could get was good enough for him; it was easier just to loaf around, sympathize with himself, and let me support the family. We brought the children home, and he looks after them. He's practically the mother now, and I'm the father! My taking a job did something to him from which he will never recover. Believe me, Dr. Popenoe, if we had to go through it again, I'd go on relief rather than take a job and let that man find out he could be supported comfortably by his wife!"

Public sentiment in some communities is unfavorable to the work of married women. A girl may lose her job on marrying, no matter how much she needs it. (On the other hand, one employer remarked, "I always like the girls in my office to marry. They do better work after that—they're so much more interested in holding on to their jobs!") Even if she can keep or get a job, all the problems will not disappear. The interference with normal parenthood is particularly serious. Nevertheless, it is often a case where the wife must work or not be a wife; and in such a case it is better for the wife to work for a while than to forego marriage or delay it indefinitely. But the difficulties should be foreseen and met intelligently.

Why Should the Parents Not Expect to Help Out?

2. *The parents may help out.* If they can afford to do so, there is every reason why they should; and it is again childish for a young man to refuse such help as might make his marriage possible, merely on the ground of what he calls "pride." When his father dies, this young man will not be too proud to take the whole estate, if it is bequeathed to him. Why should he be too proud to take part of the estate now, if it is offered?

In pioneer times, when opportunity was perhaps freer and initiative greater, it is true that public opinion tended to look down on a young man who could not or would not make his own way in the world, but had to depend on his parents. With changed conditions, public opinion is now changing.

Sometimes the parents themselves are not changing so rapidly. They may not favor having to support the young people indefinitely: they have been looking forward eagerly to getting rid of this burden, so they can have a little more leisure, or a little more luxury, or a chance to travel, or perhaps merely a chance to pay a few of their debts. Their point of view has to be taken into account. But if they are willing, the young people should not be unwilling.

3. *They can start on borrowed money.* Every argument is against this plan, except in an occasional instance where the method of repaying the loan is in sight. In that case the problem is the same as that of a business man. If he borrows on favorable terms, to repay with funds due at a definite date, which are now bringing more interest, or which will be earned by the borrowing, it is legitimate business. If he merely runs into debt to keep going, without anything but hope of getting out in some unascertainable way, he is probably headed for bankruptcy.

4. *They can go on relief.* There has been a good deal of this in the lifetimes of those who are now young people, and everyone knows of illustrations. Marie, an old acquaintance of mine, had a fairly good job. She was engaged to a man who had been on relief for several years and who, in my judgment, will continue to

be on relief for a long time to come. Marie decided that a job should not be allowed to stand in the way of true love; so she gave up the job, married the man, and they are both on relief to this day. As a taxpayer, I think that is carrying a good idea too far!

5. *Finally, they can postpone marriage indefinitely.* "I'll get a break some day," Zeke declares with forced cheerfulness, as he tries to borrow three dollars to keep up the payments on his car; while Sue, his fiancée, expresses the conviction, now somewhat dulled by four years of repetition, that "Something is sure to turn up somehow." The world is full of weak-willed drifters, lacking both imagination and determination, treading water and yelling for a rope when they need only put their feet down to find that they can touch bottom and walk ashore. Successful marriage is not for them. Even if someone paid their way, they would fail because they are failures by long practice.

Undergraduate Marriages Are Often Successful.

Marriages in college deserve a word because they represent a really new development of the last generation. When your parents were going to college, they scarcely dreamed of undergraduate marriages. Occasionally a mature man would come to college after years of work elsewhere; he might have a wife. But if a couple of ordinary juniors or seniors had announced their marriage, they would have been escorted by faculty and trustees to the edge of the campus and told, in effect, to "Go, and sin no more."

In some colleges that is still the approved treatment; but in most parts of the United States one will find several hundred married couples in the undergraduate body of any large coeducational university, and certainly several hundred unmarried couples who are earnestly canvassing the possibility of a merger. I have collected data on 252 such marriages, in which two students decided they could finish their course better married than single. "It will really be cheaper," they calculate; "and besides, we think we'll be able to concentrate better on our studies after we're married."

In only 106 of the cases did both succeed in graduating. If two students plan to marry and graduate together (or even graduate separately), they will be wise to recognize that the chances are against them. Usually, at least one has to give up study, often both. Even if there are no financial problems (thanks to their parents), the wife may become pregnant and transfer from the classroom to the delivery room. In other instances, she quits school and takes a job so that her husband may graduate and prepare himself for a better job than he could hold now. This is a legitimate investment of the wife's time, though she wants to be sure that she is investing in a sound security; for there are instances in which the wife has earned a Ph.D. or M.D. for her husband by long years of arduous work, only to have him then divorce her and marry some other girl.

Since the financial problem is almost always upper-most in the minds of these collegiate fiancés, I was especially interested in the answer to that prosaic but pertinent question, "Who paid the bills?" Almost every possible arrangement was tried, but the details could be grouped thus:

Supported by parents 110
Husband and wife both worked 72
Husband worked 53
Wife worked 17
                                                  ———
                                                  252

Sometimes the parents are by no means enthusiastic over their contributions but try, as they would express it, to make the best of a bad bargain. In other cases, their sympathy and helpfulness leave nothing to be desired, from the point of view of the young married couple.

How did these marriages turn out? Those listed as happy numbered 191, with 23 doubtful and 38 definitely unhappy. Some of these marriages were forced by the pregnancy of the girl, or by other factors that would hardly be expected to contribute to the happiness of the household. Moreover, most of them were fairly recent.* But that 76 per cent of them were

* I have data as to the duration of marriage for only 172 of these, ranging from a few months to fifteen years: only one-fourth of them were of more than five years' standing. Within these limits there was no tendency for the marriages to deteriorate with age. For the benefit of the statistically-trained reader, I mention that when happiness was correlated with duration of marriage, bi-serial $r = .10 \pm .07$ and tetrachoric $r = .12$.

classed as definitely happy speaks well for the intelligence of the partners.

Certainly most college students have plenty to do without adding the responsibilities of matrimony. Most of them are not so mature emotionally that they need feel under any strong compulsion to conjugate themselves at once. Most of them will be well advised to finish their college work, get jobs, and prepare deliberately to start a home. But if an occasional couple are unusually mature, if they can meet the financial difficulties, if they are certain that they "have found each other", and if they have the character and determination to go through, they need not necessarily be discouraged. They will probably face some serious difficulties; but they might have more to face if they did not marry, and they might at the same time lose some of the years of happiness to which they are entitled if they want to work for happiness.

In any case, money is not a major factor in the success of marriage.[130] Sages have long preached, and occasionally practiced, the virtues of poverty; but no reasonable man would believe that poverty was any particular help to success in marriage. Statistically, however, it is no particular hindrance, either.

Of course it is almost impossible to get people to believe this. "Economic difficulties" constitute one of the stock items in lists of the ostensible causes for divorce. Many people firmly believe that economic difficulty wrecks more homes than does any other one cause. It is hard to get such people to realize, for instance, that the depression which began in 1929 helped as many families as it hurt: yet that is not far from the truth.[3] Weak families might be broken by it; but strong families might be brought closer together, might learn to co-operate more effectively, might find new resources in their own companionship.[14]

Every competent study yet made, so far as I know, yields the same conclusion: that there is statistically no relation between the income of a family and its happiness [11, 108] (or between the income of an unmarried person and his happiness,[124] for that matter). One couple starts with nothing and makes a success of marriage. Another couple starts with everything that friends and relatives can think of; they, just as much as the former couple, are "two souls with but a single thought, two hearts that beat as one"; but in six months the single thought of these two souls is how to beat each other. The difference is not in the amount of money in the bank, but in the amount of character in the partners.

It would be irresponsible to advise young people to marry when they have no means of support; but it is equally unrealistic to advise them to wait indefinitely with the hope that maybe, by and by, everything will be lovely. If they are mature, and if they have anything at all to work with, they will often do better to join forces and work their problems out together. Most young people need more money than they have; but some young people need also, much more urgently, a greater amount of faith and work.

CHAPTER XV

THE PREMARITAL EXAMINATION

MANY states now require some sort of examination of one or both partners before a marriage license is issued. The chief purpose of this is to prevent the spread of infectious diseases, particularly of the venereal diseases. It is a good precaution so far as it goes, and anyone who proposes to evade such a law by going into another state for a license lays himself open to strong suspicion, if not of trying to cover up something, then at least of a lack of good citizenship.

But these laws are unfortunately not yet universal, and at best they do not go as far as is desirable. No intelligent person should stop with a mere "blood test"; every couple before marriage should get the most comprehensive and skilful examination possible. Physicians who are prepared to be of special help in this way are not to be found everywhere; but more and more medical men are taking an interest in the subject, and if one has no "family physician", a little inquiry will usually locate one who can be of service. In the absence of any other indication, try to locate a man who has graduated from a well-known medical college—one attached to some large university, for instance, who came out not more than ten or fifteen years ago, so that he is young enough to have modern ideas. In larger communities, a man should seek a urologist or specialist in genito-urinary diseases, a woman should go to a gynecologist or obstetrician, unless there is some reason for seeking another expert. Incidentally, many physicians are very reasonable in their charges for pre-marital examinations, feeling that it is a useful public service and also, no doubt, that it is a good time to make friends.

Even a rather ordinary examination offers a number of great advantages to either a man or a woman:

1. *It helps to dispel mere ignorance.* Many people who are supposed to be well educated have an almost unbelievable ignorance of the anatomy and physiology of reproduction. Think over all the things you would like to know, make a memorandum of them, and ask the doctor to correct or confirm your ideas. Of course you will have read some of the many good books and pamphlets now widely available, but there may still be some points to clear up.

2. *It reassures you as to your normality.* Many young men have more or less absurd ideas on this point. Given no satisfactory and natural instruction, they have brooded over hints, over the meaning of jokes they have heard, over the implications of patent-medicine advertisements. They have convinced themselves that they are peculiar in some way—that their reproductive organs are abnormally small, for instance. Even at this late day, it is helpful to have such nonsense dispelled.

It is worth while to emphasize here that almost all

of the supposed sex abnormalities which weigh on the minds of young men are wholly imaginary. Worry about "lost manhood" as a result of seminal emissions is quite unnecessary. Such nocturnal emissions ("wet dreams") are not merely a natural but a healthful experience.

Many a man when he has attempted to have intercourse with a prostitute, finds his consort so repugnant to him, or he is so displeased with the circumstances, that he is completely impotent. This does not at all mean that he will be impotent in marriage.

Importance of Freedom From
Venereal Diseases.

3. *It certifies to your freedom from infectious disease.* While many other illnesses may be important in marriage (see Chapter VII), state laws are correct in promoting the idea that syphilis and gonorrhea are for practical purposes the ones most to be taken into account.

Syphilis is a killing disease which affects perhaps 10 per cent of the entire American population at some time during life. Sexual intercourse outside of marriage is the main source of infection, directly or indirectly (indirectly when many innocent wives and children pay the penalty, not for their own mistakes but for those of a husband or father). It can be transmitted by kissing, by the use of unclean instruments in a barber shop, by an insufficiently washed glass at a restaurant or soda fountain, and in similar ways. Such accidental infections are not common enough to justify anyone in becoming panicky; but they emphasize the fact that the venereal diseases are not to be regarded merely as just and proper punishment for sinful persons! They are the concern of the whole community.

With pneumonia, cancer, and heart disease, syphilis is one of the great killers in modern civilization; and, in addition, it is responsible for more than 10 per cent of all insanity, through infection of the brain. Its relation to marriage is of most concern to this book, however. The common history is that a man has acquired syphilis from some prostitute—professional or amateur —early in life; thinks he is cured, or hopes he is; marries, and promptly infects his wife. The result may be miscarriages and stillbirths. Syphilis is the greatest single cause of miscarriages in some parts of the population; and a large proportion of the offspring of untreated syphilitic mothers die either before birth or in the first year of life. Those who survive despite infection are the so-called "congenital or pre-natal syphilitics" who, even though they live to maturity, never have a healthy day. Routine tests of all pregnant women, and prompt treatment for those found to need it, are now reducing this toll.

Syphilis usually begins with a small sore on the genitals; and if it is treated by a competent physician as soon as this appears, it can usually be stopped. If this is not done, the germs pass into the blood within a few weeks, and it then takes years to get rid of them; indeed, it is sometimes impossible. A cure often depends on several years of faithful subjection to skilful treatment; inexpert handling may result in death or something worse.

It is out of the question for a man who has ever had syphilis to become engaged, much less married, until he *knows* he is cured; and the premarital examination is much too late for him to ascertain this; but it does serve as a final precaution and as an evidence of good faith. This is much too important for anyone to expect a partner to take it for granted.

Gonorrhea, the other important venereal disease, is more frequent than syphilis, but is a crippling rather than a killing infection. It is fairly easy to cure if taken under treatment by an expert immediately after infection. Much of the damage done by it results from the idea spread among men that "a dose of clap is no worse than a bad cold," and to self-treatment by patent medicines. By the injection of these astringent solutions, a man may dry up the discharge from the urethra, at the same time forcing the germs farther back into his body, where they become established in bladder or scrotum, or even in his joints, and can perhaps never be eradicated.

The man who contemplates becoming engaged and who has ever had gonorrhea, no matter how long ago, should submit himself to prolonged tests by the best doctor in town, not by one of the benevolent gentlemen who prints his picture in the papers with upraised hand, exclaiming, "MEN, I KNOW YOUR TROUBLES!"

Probably no man ever had gonorrhea without knowing that something was the matter with him, because of the inflammation of the urethra and pain accompanying urination. It is not only possible but common for a woman to have gonorrhea without knowing it, and to infect a man when she has not the slightest idea that she is infectious.

The man who marries, merely *thinking* that he is cured, may infect his wife. Gonorrhea in the female is hard to cure; it may work its way up from the vagina into the uterus and fallopian tubes, producing sterility and occasionally death through peritonitis. It has in the past been one of the common causes of blindness in children; but obstetricians now take pains, as a matter of routine, to disinfect the eyes of the newborn baby, lest he have gotten germs into them while being squeezed through the birth canal.

It is not necessary to go into further details to show that gonorrhea, far from being a mild and amusing episode, is one of the most serious plagues affecting the world; and the worst thing about it, perhaps, is that the chief sufferers are so often wives and babies, innocent of all wrong-doing and the victims of a husband who *thought* he was cured and would perhaps rather have died than have infected his family.

The remedy is, first, to avoid infection (which means, practically, to avoid sexual intercourse outside of marriage); second, if ever infected, to make absolutely certain of cure before marriage. The laws of many states, requiring a certificate of freedom from disease, or the so-called blood test (Wassermann test), do not provide adequate examination for gonorrhea; they are aimed primarily at syphilis. It is therefore all the more necessary for one who plans to marry to consult a competent advisor and have a full examination made on his own account.

The treatment of venereal diseases has made extraordinary progress in recent years through the introduction of such compounds as sulfanilimide for gonorrhea; but not every patient can take this. The heat treatment, creating an artificial fever in the patient by raising his body temperature to about 106° F., also produces remarkable results in some chronic cases of syphilis and gonorrhea, but is so strenuous that only about one in four of those who need the treatment is able to endure it. Avoidance of infection is still a safe policy.

4. *The premarital examination gives a final opportunity to consult an authority* on any question pertaining to your heredity or that of your fiancée. These questions should have been settled, so far as you are concerned, before you asked any girl to marry you; but if new evidence has come to light, it may now be weighed.

5. *It permits both partners to get, at the last moment, any assistance necessary* to make successful sexual adjustments (see Chapter XVII). In this respect the examination is of much more value to the woman than to the man, since there are more conditions in woman

than in man knowledge of which in advance may prevent at least embarrassment if not serious difficulty in getting a proper start in marriage. To one who knows how often something of this sort is brought to light in examination by a competent gynecologist, it is almost incredible that any intelligent woman is willing to marry without a premarital examination.

Get Expert Advice About Contraception.

6. *It gives a chance to get the most authentic information on contraception.* Most young couples want to delay the arrival of the first baby for at least a year or two. Sometimes this seems a financial necessity. Everyone should know, however, that there is no one hundred per cent dependable method of birth control; there is none that is foolproof; there is none that works as well for inexperienced persons as for those who are accustomed to its use. There is no method that does not have some drawbacks, including esthetic and financial drawbacks. Moreover, no one method is equally suitable for all persons, or for the same person at all ages.

It is therefore a mistake to take the advice of the first druggist interviewed, or to have some married man assure you that "This has always worked for my wife." Perhaps his wife is sterile anyway!

Of the various methods before the public, it may be said at once that the so-called "safe period" is not safe.

Biologists generally agree that an egg-cell is most likely to be liberated from the ovary about half way between two menstrual periods. If no egg-cell has been liberated within the last few days before coitus, or will be liberated within the succeeding few days, conception will not take place. But it is well established that an egg-cell may be liberated at other times of the month, and that women vary greatly in this respect as in others. While intercourse in the week before the beginning of menstruation is less likely to result in pregnancy than at any other time, this is not a completely sterile period.

If two persons have strong religious objections to the use of any mechanical or chemical contraceptive, they may use the "safe period" as better than nothing, and as at least tending to diminish the likelihood of conception. But it need hardly be said that a plan which forces a young husband and wife to conduct their love-life according to the calendar, instead of according to their feelings, is objectionable.

Since there is no "best" method of contraception, no one standard procedure to be recommended to all persons, the intelligent move is to call on the examining physician for expert help at the time of the premarital examination, and then for this particular couple to adopt the method that seems most desirable at the time for them.

In general, however, a method used by the husband should be preferred to one used by the wife. It is important that the husband, from the first, should have a feeling of responsibility for the comfort and happiness of his wife. This is a good way in which to show it.

In addition to these advantages which the premarital examinations offers to both sexes, the woman has particular opportunities to profit by it. In addition to those already noted are:

1. A competent examiner can note indications of sterility or low fertility and suggest means of dealing with them. Some glandular disturbances are recognized without much difficulty. Obesity is often associated with sterility; but the fat girl may not get to the examiner, since men tend to discriminate against her in marriage. (If she does marry, and is more than fifteen pounds overweight, statistical studies show that she may be less happy than the average in marriage.[11])

Sterility may also be the result of a previous abortion which has produced an inflammation that closed and sealed the fallopian tubes. The number of abortions on unmarried women is much smaller than is generally supposed. While exact figures are not to be had, it is guessed that of all abortions, nine tenths are performed on married women, largely on women who already have several children and have put too much reliance in their contraceptive methods. Any young woman who has had an abortion should have a thorough examination, including inflation of the tubes with air to find out whether they are open, before she is betrothed— not just a few weeks before she expects to marry. Abortion is a much more serious procedure, from a biological point of view, than is generally supposed: its death-rate is many times that of normal childbirth, and it may result in lifelong infection, in sterility, or in a partial unsexing of the woman due to the disturbance of her endocrine glands.[106]

2. The examination will bring to light any unusual condition such as narrow pelvis, that may affect child-bearing. The girl who is forewarned in such matters will be able to plan intelligently and will know what sort of help she needs and where to find it when she needs it.

3. There is also a distinct advantage to many women in a physical examination to "de-sensitize" them slightly, if one may use the expression. Many girls who are otherwise well educated, still have abnormal fears concerning sex and an abnormal sensitivity concerning their own reproductive organs. An impersonal and scientific examination by a gynecologist, preferably a man, helps to remove some of the unreasonable prudery and squeamishness of such girls.

Any premarital examination is better than none. The more thorough, the better; and it is desirable that it include not merely an inspection of the reproductive organs and certification of freedom from infectious disease, but also a study of the personal and family history and the personality of the partners. The premarital service of the American Institute of Family Relations [74] includes a battery of standard psychological tests that measure such traits as emotional maturity, neurotic tendencies, introversion or extraversion, self-sufficiency or dependence, dominance or submissiveness, and present adjustment to one's home, work, and social life. Such an inventory (which could be given by any psychologist

at slight expense) helps the individual to know his own
nature and that of his partner. Any combination of
traits is compatible with success in marriage, but it is
highly desirable that those concerned should know what
the combination is. Anyone can play the game of life
more intelligently if he knows what cards he holds in
his hand. If he also knows in advance what cards his
partner holds, he ought to win!

CHAPTER XVI

THE WEDDING

THERE are four ways in which one can marry in the United States:

1. *By a religious ceremony,* which is performed by some duly ordained clergyman. This requires a license.

2. *By a civil ceremony,* performed by a justice of the peace or some equivalent official. This also requires a license.

3. *By contract.* In some states two persons can enter into marriage just as they would enter into a business partnership, by having a legal contract drawn and signing it in the presence of some designated official, such as the judge of one of the more important courts. This usually requires a marriage license, also. The arrangement is favored by those who, because of their religious views or other reasons, object to "having someone else marry them." No third party, they allege, can make them man and wife; it is they who take each other for this purpose. Such procedures are rare.

4. *By common law.* In one third or more of the states of the union, the mere fact of living together creates a presumption of marriage; and even though there has been neither license nor ceremony, either party can ask the state to recognize this as in fact a marriage and the

offspring (if any) as legitimate. This marriage by mutual consent without any formalities was common in the Middle Ages and was brought to this continent by the early English settlers. It was abolished in England in 1753, but has survived here to be a continual source of blackmail and notoriety. It should have been abolished long ago. It is hard to imagine conditions under which any person with self-respect or respect for his wife would take advantage of it.

In actual practice a choice is made almost invariably between a religious ceremony of some kind and a wedding before the justice of the peace. Three fourths of the marriages in America are in the former group, one fourth in the latter. The proportion depends on the socio-economic level; with the most church marriages among the professional and business classes, while the skilled and unskilled labor groups have proportionately more marriages by a justice of the peace.[83] Doubtless there are many reasons. The "upper classes" may be prone to make at least a greater outward show of conservatism and conventionality. The church wedding gives opportunity, if desired, for a much greater social display; and this group can afford it while the less-favored group can not. Moreover, marriages in the laboring group are made on shorter acquaintance, and perhaps a little less formality is involved at every point.

These differences in the background and personality of the people involved also help to explain why church marriages turn out more successfully than others.[23]

Though they comprise three fourths of the weddings, they account for only two thirds of the divorces.[94] There is probably a real advantage in the more formal ceremony; it creates a psychological effect favorable to taking the whole matter seriously; and freak marriages (in an airplane or submarine; in the lion's cage or on a platform at the county fair)—all attempts, in short, to turn the wedding into a vaudeville performance—should long since have been outlawed by Protestant churches. A good illustration was furnished by the newspapers as this chapter was written: To celebrate Cherry Day in a certain town, a couple were to be married while standing up to their waists in a vat of cherry juice!

However, the main difference probably lies in the greater tendency toward conservatism of those who are married in churches; and in the fact that in this group there is likely to be more economic pressure to hold the couple together. On the one hand, there may be property interests; on the other hand, the wife in this group may not be so ready to go out and take an unskilled job and support herself after divorce; she may therefore work a little harder to make the marriage a success.

June is the month of traditional preference for weddings in the United States and Canada, but a survey [117] of other countries shows it is not universally favored. Agricultural countries have most weddings in the fall, after the harvest is in; and in the United States the preferred months, next to June, are September and October. The hottest months and the coldest months alike are avoided, the least popular months in order named being March, January, and August in the United States. Two and one-half times as many marriage licenses are issued in June as in March—although the latter is the longer month!

Notoriously, the man in the case frequently has little to say about the circumstances of the wedding. These are controlled ostensibly by the girl, but in practice largely by her female relatives, who flock from near and far to take part. Whether he approves of what is being done or not, the average man consoles himself with the fact that there is nothing he can do about it; that the whole business is not worth fighting over; and that even if it is a nuisance it will not last long; and, after all, he can afford to pay the price—the girl is worth it. He lets her set the exact date of the wedding, of course, not merely for her convenience in other respects, but to fit into her menstrual cycle. She will naturally try to avoid being married just before she expects to menstruate.

Secret Marriages Have Many Disadvantages.

While the average wedding is a more or less formal affair in proportion to the tastes and finances of the families involved, there are also many secret marriages and elopements of all sorts, for a variety of reasons. The clamor raised in recent years against allowing a married woman to work for pay outside the home has put a premium on either secret marriages or common-law marriages. In most states a married woman will not be hired as a teacher; and if a teacher marries, she will lose her job. I have known of several instances in which a teacher married secretly and concealed the fact either until she had finished the school year, or, occasionally, for several years, until she felt that she could afford to relinquish her salary—or until she became pregnant. The same thing may happen in various state and governmental services which discriminate against married women.

The attempt to prevent married women from working is based largely on the argument that their husbands can support them and that there should not be two jobs in any one family, when jobs are scarce; the married woman should turn over her salary to some unmarried person who needs it more. Whatever may be the economic merits of the practice (in my opinion they are often demerits), it is clear that society does not gain by discouraging marriage, putting a premium on sexual partnerships outside of marriage, or forcing husbands and wives to live under disheartening and sometimes degrading conditions of concealment.

Sometimes men and women deliberately choose this course, preferring a "free love" mating to a wedding. In some circles there is talk about marriage as a cramping and confining affair, a deprivation of liberty. "Love" should not be forced into bonds, it is averred. In answer, one might ask just what marriage really is? A moment's thought will show that it is merely the partnership of two mature and responsible (to ascertain this is the purpose of the license) persons who are publicly, that is, in the presence of witnesses (this is the essence of the wedding ceremony), declaring that they are taking each other as man and wife, and that they are willing to accept the consequences. Can society ask any less than this? Should anyone want to give any less? Avoidance of a license raises a strong presumption that people are not mature and responsible; avoidance of a wedding raises a strong presumption that they are not willing to avow the relationship because they are not willing to accept the consequences. Surely there is nothing very advanced, progressive, or "modern" about a partnership of which one of the outstanding characteristics is insistence on irresponsibility! If civilization needs anything, it needs a greater feeling of individual responsibility—in industry, in politics, in trade, in finance, in parenthood, as well as in marriage. To deprive sexual partnerships of the protection afforded by a formal wedding is to go back to the animal level.

Living together without marriage is therefore no solution of anyone's problems; and a secret wedding is a very unsatisfactory solution, as well. While lecturing in universities I am sometimes consulted by young couples who want to know whether they cannot profitably enter into a secret marriage. Each has a year or two of undergraduate work ahead. They are betrothed, although the fact may not have been announced publicly. Their parents, who are supporting them in college, will not consent to a marriage now. Perhaps they

have sounded out their parents on this point and have
been told, "If you want to marry now, go ahead—
but don't expect us to support you. You will have to
take care of yourselves after that." This may be an
unreasonable attitude on the part of the parents, or it
may not be; but it is their attitude. What are the young
people going to do? They cannot help imagining that
they might marry secretly and be together whenever
they can, at least occasionally; and since the parents
would know nothing of this arrangement, they would
continue the allowances. After graduation, husband
and wife could confront their respective families with,
"Here we are. We put it over on you!"

Usually they have not thought through the problem
at all. How are they going to be together as they desire? It involves constant deception, constant fear of
detection, constant sneaking down the alley and up
the fire escape, so to speak. Marriage is too fine a thing
to be put on that basis!

Harold and Francine had the advantage of going to
college a thousand miles from their homes. In their
senior year they married and began housekeeping, but
were considerate enough not to mention the fact to
any of their relatives. The allowances continued to
come each month, and they lived comfortably on their
joint bank account, although neither would have received a cent if their respective parents had suspected
the marriage. The couple now have two children of
their own in college; their married life has been ideal,
even though its start was clouded by deceit; but

neither set of parents has ever accepted the situation emotionally, and the hard feeling that has existed for twenty years makes a high price to pay for their few extra months of conjugal life.

A Study of the Results of Elopement.

To get a better view of secret marriages and elopements, I studied 738 of them, details of which were collected by my students at various times. They could be classified roughly in five groups, according to motivation:[92]

1. *Parental objection.* This is the "classical" type, but accounts for only 46 per cent of the total. Often my sympathies were with the young people, not with the parents. The latter sometimes appeared in a contemptible rôle. On the other hand, some of the marriages had little back of them.

Aloysius and Elaine were fellow students who ran away to a near-by town and were married. They returned the same day and went their own ways until Elaine could break the news to her father, who was a Kloncatenated Klonstitutional Kleagle of the Ku Klux Klan, or something of the sort, and who, she feared, might not overflow with paternal affection when he learned that his daughter had espoused a fellow who was at least nominally a Roman Catholic. The anticipated time when the father would be in a mellow mood never arrived, and the marriage was never consummated.

They graduated, drifted apart, and when I met Aloysius, seven years after this wedding, he had not even heard of, much less from, his "wife in name only" for nearly six years. Obviously, such episodes are of no value to anyone concerned.

Of the secret marriages motivated by parental objection, 45 per cent turned out happily.

2. *Publicity*—to avoid it, or get it. This group includes the school teachers and others who might have been discharged had their marriages been known, and who could not afford just at that time, they thought, to bid farewell to the payroll. But there are others who have more or less legitimate reasons to avoid publicity. In several instances one of the parties had just been divorced and wanted to prevent comment.

Eustace and Grace had been engaged for a year when the former was arrested on a charge of defrauding his employer. As he came of a prominent family in their small city, his trial was accompanied by abundant notoriety. He was completely exonerated, but they decided to marry as secretly as possible and start life in another state, to avoid further gossip.

While some elope to avoid publicity, others do so to acquire it. It has become almost a custom in the motion picture colony of Hollywood and in the broad fringe of its imitators to "elope" by airplane to Arizona or Nevada as a means of getting a little extra publicity in the newspapers. Various fourth-rate airports have billboards advertising a special service for this purpose.

Lionel and Hildegarde had been going together, off

and on, for four years. They had announced an engagement several times, and then dissolved it. One evening they met a friend in whose company they absorbed some impure diluted ethyl alcohol. The friend became expansive. "Look here," he said to them. "You two have been going together long enough. You're going to get married some day; why don't you do it tonight and get it over with? I know where we can get an airplane; I'll pay for a trip to Nevada and go along with you to see fair play." The marriage dragged along for a few months until, in spite of the fact that Hildegarde was pregnant, she left Lionel and got a divorce five weeks before the child was born.

One in every five of the elopements I studied could be referred to this "matter of publicity" group. The fact that 60 per cent of them turned out happily shows that some, at least, had legitimate reasons for the act.

3. *Economy* was the motive in one out of every eight of the elopements.

Mamie's parents thought they ought to give her an elaborate wedding. She knew they could not afford it; so she persuaded Nathan to marry her unexpectedly, and thus solved the problem.

In the case of Oliver and Marian, the gears did not enmesh. Facing exactly the same situation, they sneaked off to a neighboring town and were married. When they returned and realized how much a big show meant to all the relatives on both sides, they could not bring themselves to break the news; so they went ahead and were married all over again with a big show.

Marjorie's parents were not well-to-do, but she had a rich aunt who called her in and handed her a check for $500. "Now, my dear," auntie assured her, "I want you to take this and have just the kind of a wedding you'd like to have. If there's anything left over, put it in the bank." Marjorie and Ted conferred long and earnestly, finally slipped over into an adjoining county, were married by a justice of the peace at a total cost of $5, and returned to start housekeeping. The first item in their new budget book was: "Balance on hand, $495."

On the whole, however, people who are foresighted and thrifty are likely to be the kind of people who succeed in marriage, or in any other enterprise; and the success of the economy group, 63 per cent, is greater than that of any other group in my study.

4. *Pregnancy*. The hasty marriage necessitated by the girl's pregnancy is an old story, usually an unpleasant one; not the least objectionable feature being the fact that the husband so often, in future quarrels, reminds his wife that he only married her because he had to. We have had to deal with the aftermath of so many of these, at the American Institute of Family Relations, that we have strong convictions about the management of the betrothal period (see Chapter XII). In the 738 elopements here considered, however, there were only fifty-eight pregnancy cases, or 8 per cent of the total. Two thirds of them turned out failures, but in some cases this had been virtually foreseen, the marriage being intended primarily to legitimize the child, with the expectation that a divorce would be got later. It is a poor

sort of marriage. One could hardly say, however, that letting the child come into the world with the unjust stigma of bastardy was socially preferable.

5. *Miscellaneous cases,* not easily ascribed to any of the other groups, made a final group comprising 14 per cent of the whole. Many of these were drunks; in some instances they had been victimized by other persons who hoped to profit by the marriage.

One of my students had worked in a garage on the road between San Francisco and Nevada. One evening a car drew up containing Elbert and Emma, half drunk and on the road to Reno for an elopement, and Emma's sister Lizzie, two thirds drunk, who had gone along because she didn't want to miss the fun and refused to be left behind. While the carburetor was being adjusted, Lizzie implored my student to come along with them and marry her; they could just as well make it a four-some, she declared. Whether Lizzie found any more willing groom between Placerville and Reno I do not know; but I cite the case as an illustration of the slender basis on which some hasty marriages rest, as well as an argument for a three-day delay before a license is issued!

Of these miscellaneous secret marriages, 39 per cent turned out well. Of the 738 elopements, altogether, 48 per cent were successful so far as known. The details serve to document the general knowledge that there are all sorts of reasons for eloping, some good and some bad, and that the success of the marriage depends not so much on the nature of the ceremony as on the quality of the people who enter into it.

In general, however, a formal wedding, simple as one desires but at least preannounced, publicly avowed, and destitute of all buffoonery, seems to be a desirable preparation for successful married life.

CHAPTER XVII

THE BEGINNING OF MARRIED LIFE

THE wedding is over, and immemorial custom leads the young couple to seek seclusion for a short period, during which they may make a start in the new and intimate relationship which will control their lives henceforth. This honeymoon may be either a keynote to a symphony of marriage or a series of blunders to be lived down with difficulty. It calls for just as much intelligent management as any other phase of marriage.

Do not commence by turning it into a sight-seeing tour, or a parade to exhibit your bride to all the relatives who were too decrepit to attend the wedding. The combination of physical, mental, and emotional strain is often a severe tax on the bride; perhaps on the groom, too. Do not spend all your nights on Pullman cars. Find some peaceful resort with inspiring surroundings, perhaps at the seaside or in the mountains. Give your time over to getting acquainted with each other quietly: loaf and invite your souls, and return home refreshed and rejuvenated.

In the next place, remember that from a biological point of view your personal status has not been changed by the wedding ceremony. Do not go ahead as if the function of the wedding was to give you legal ownership of your bride. The ceremony, as I have emphasized in the preceding chapter, is merely notice to whom it may concern that the two contracting parties intend to enter upon the state of matrimony; which state, affecting many other than themselves, naturally demands that they acknowledge publicly their intentions and responsibility.

Biologically, the physical consummation is the real marriage, and it would be well if the wedding and the marriage were more clearly distinguished in popular thought. Theoretically, from this point of view, the wedding ceremony might take place at any time prior to the marriage. The marriage itself, if it has the greatest possible value, can take place only when husband and wife, having made previous declaration of intention, are mutually ready for and desirous of it.

If a man's wooing has been skillful and his bride well brought up, she will doubtless be prepared to have the marriage on the night following the wedding or, better still, on the succeeding day. But it must not be taken for granted that she is ready, emotionally, even though she doubtless will be ready intellectually.

Even under the most favorable conditions, a man should not expect success at his first attempt to consummate the marriage. Though she be gladly receiving him and passionately endeavoring to give herself up to him, the bride often finds that the resistance of her muscles, ruled by an unconscious mechanism that has been trained to resistance throughout her entire life, is wholly beyond her voluntary control and can be dissolved only gradually. But patience, tenderness, and continuous wooing by her mate will succeed soon enough.

Beyond that, the husband must remember that only in a minority of cases does his wife receive from the first union the pleasure that she anticipates. Study of records [108] which the American Institute of Family Relations collected from hundreds of married couples showed that of every four brides, one experienced an orgasm at first intercourse, one after some days or weeks, one after a period varying from one to eleven months; one only after a year, if ever.

Naturally, few husbands have as much difficulty in reaching an orgasm, but many of them find the first experience disappointing; they are not proud of themselves. In such circumstances, it is all too easy for each to blame the other. Much trouble can be avoided if husband and wife at this time will bear in mind, as always, that successful sex life in marriage is never something attained at a single bound. It is a gradual development. Sex life is more perfect the second week than the first week; more perfect the second year than the first year; and so it progresses, indefinitely.

Part of the bride's difficulty comes from actual pain at the first intercourse. Some of this is usually associated with the hymen, the slight membrane which partly closes the entrance to the vagina. This should be stretched slowly; and if the bride has had a competent examination before marriage, her physician will have shown her how she herself can stretch it. If it is unusually thick or resistant, he will have taken the necessary measures to deal with it. If the hymen is stretched suddenly and forcibly, its edges will be nicked, giving rise to a slight bleeding.

The hymen, like other vestigial and now useless parts of the human anatomy, is extremely variable.[58] Sometimes it is so heavy that intercourse is impossible without the help of a surgeon; on the other hand it may be so slight as scarcely to be detected even by a gynecologist; and it may be so easily stretched that a woman may give birth to a child and still have an intact hymen. Rare though such cases are, they should be borne in mind. The absence of bleeding at the first intercourse is by no means conclusive proof that the woman is not a virgin.

This is the time for the husband to be a gentleman as well as a *gentle man;* not the time for him to conduct pseudo-scientific investigations to determine whether he married a virgin. All studies available indicate that, in the educated part of the population, the great majority of women enter marriage without previous experience of sexual intercourse. So much sensational nonsense is published on this point by irresponsible magazines that it is just as well to stop occasionally and recall the facts:

It is generally recognized that during and after the World War there was a let-down in ethical standards. War is an abnegation of all morality, and it is not to be supposed that its effects can be kept in water-tight compartments. Young people who went through late adolescence during and shortly after the World War show somewhat greater history of extra-marital relationships—though the available data are fragmentary. Since then, a few studies on sophisticated groups, selected in such a way as probably to get an undue proportion of neurotics, show one girl in every four having had sexual intercourse before marriage; [10] but the bulk of studies available indicate that the number of educated wives who have ever had any sexual experience except with their husbands is more like one in fifteen,[34] or one in thirty.[17] Both in the college world [5] and in the world of business and industry,[6] the attitudes of young women as well as of young men are now surprisingly conservative, and their ideals biologically sound. The next time someone tells you the contrary, ask him for what the lawyers call a "bill of particulars."

If, in the case now under consideration, the wife is one of the small minority who have had previous sexual experience, the husband probably knows it. If not, he does not need to make things any harder for her; let him put the matter out of his mind and never refer to it. If his wife has made unwise experiments in the past, she will probably pay a high penalty for it in the memory of sordid episodes that crowds in on her when she wants single-mindedly to give herself up to her own husband; and the man, if he has had premarital sexual experience, will punish himself in exactly the same way—nothing that he can do now will enable him to avoid this punishment.

A variety of studies [17, 29, 108] made by different investigators for different reasons all agree in showing that the happiest marriages are between two persons, neither of whom has had any previous sexual experience. If the husband, because of experiments in the past, is so unfortunate as to have prejudiced his opportunity to make his marriage unique, he should do his best to forget all he has ever learned and start over again. Sexual partnership in marriage is wholly mutual—a sharing. Intercourse with a prostitute is as far from this as could be imagined. It represents a wholly selfish seeking, on the part of the man, for his own gratification; and the man who enters matrimony in this spirit is doomed from the start.

Sexual intercourse* is only a part of the general pattern of marriage, of complete partnership. It must be fitted into the pattern of community living: a difficult job if either one, through premature and immature experiments, has learned to regard it, not as an integral part of a complete union, but merely as an isolated and exciting episode somewhat comparable to a ride on a roller coaster. To the extent that husband and wife establish a really co-operative partnership *in everything*, their sex life will be valuable.

Two Theories Concerning the Management of Marriage.

There are two general theories of conduct, largely opposed to each other, regarding daily life in marriage.

---

* A detailed discussion of the technique of coitus would exceed the space of this chapter. I have dealt with the subject fully in a 24-page pamphlet on "Preparing for Marriage," which can be had for 25 cents from the American Institute of Family Relations, Los Angeles.

One is that the partners should have everything in common: share the same bed, never go out separately, have no secrets from each other; in short, be as nearly one as possible. The other is that partners should maintain almost as much individuality and reserve as before they were married: should occupy separate beds or preferably separate rooms, should cultivate distinct circles of friends, take their vacations apart, and in general avoid the effects of too great intimacy—effects which are supposed to destroy the glamour and lead to disillusionment and satiety.

In the light of Chapter IX, I think it will be evident that when the latter policy is carried to an extreme it is merely a manifestation of an infantile, often neurotic, outlook on life. Marriage is a free relationship. Two people who go into marriage can make of it anything they please. They can live in one room and never let each other out of sight, or they can live ten thousand miles apart and be together only on Christmas. It is their marriage, and society does not particularly care how they work it out, so long as they comply with the indispensable preliminary of accepting responsibility for their own actions. It is all a matter of taste; yet these questions of taste might well be interpreted with the aid of intelligence.

Consider the plan of separateness more fully. The advantages claimed for it are that it maintains the attraction of novelty, of inaccessibility, which is supposed to be particularly stimulating to the male sex; that it puts a keener edge on such pleasures as the two enjoy in common; and that, as each partner sees the other only at his or her best, the glamour never wears off and the halo does not dim.

Some of these advantages are real, but the drawbacks are no less real. Having a maximum of separate interests and a minimum of interests in common, the two naturally tend to emphasize the former and gradually to drift away from each other. Shortly they are explaining to their friends that a divorce seems the only thing: they will always respect each other, but "We really haven't anything in common!" Why should they have anything in common unless they try to have something in common?

If the wife is at all inclined to be unresponsive or unduly reserved, or if the husband is not wholly the poetic lover that she thinks he should be, the resulting situation (a common one among occupants of twin beds!) is that intimacy and wooing occur mainly, or only, when the husband seeks sexual union with his wife. This gradually builds up in her mind the idea (not altogether incorrect) that his greatest interest in her is for his own physical gratification. Thus the two keep drifting farther apart, in body and in spirit, until a definite split comes.

The advantages claimed for the first-named plan of complete intimacy are that it gives the two the greatest possible fund of common interests, emphasizes at every point their nearness to each other—mentally as well as physically—and encourages them to develop along similar lines instead of in opposite directions. These are all real advantages, but partly counterbalanced if the intimacy of daily life results in too great carelessness about personal appearance or in a coarsening of the more delicate phases of companionship.

The true line of procedure for most people lies between these two plans, although nearer to that of intimacy than to that of separation. It ought not to be necessary (but unfortunately it is, most emphatically!) to insist on the maintenance of personal neatness, and the most scrupulous cleanliness of every part of the body. A woman likes to feel that her body is admired by her lover; he should not fail to give her occasion for this. Privacy may also be recognized for the more personal aspects of the toilet, but it should not be allowed to degenerate into a neurotic squeamishness.

A crucial illustration is furnished by the sleeping accommodations. Since the dawn of history, married people have almost universally preferred to sleep together. It is only of late years that a movement in the opposite direction has been pronounced. This apparently began in the leisure class, where having two beds, or even separate rooms, was looked upon as a mark of distinction from the common herd. In late years the movement has been assiduously furthered by furniture dealers, who get twice as much money from the sale of two beds as of one, and who therefore have an understandable reason for pushing the innovation by every means in their power. It was fostered for some years by a false and squeamish idea of delicacy (now fortunately disappearing) which made people ashamed to admit that they enjoyed sleeping together and refused to be deprived of this delight. It may have been favored by some women as a defense against ignorant or inconsiderate husbands. It is occasionally demanded by a partner who, more or less neurotic, alleges that he cannot sleep well except alone.

With all this to promote the innovation, it has never become the rule. A survey [108] of middle-class married couples in California showed that only one out of every four occupied twin beds. Since most of the population below the middle class holds to the double bed for economy if for no other reason, it is evident that only a small minority of the population occupies twin beds; and the custom seems to be losing ground steadily in spite of the exertions of the furniture dealers. Its disappearance would be an advantage. Many biologists have always looked upon it as fundamentally undesirable; Auguste Forel went so far as seriously to question the permanence of love between occupants of twin beds. Such beds inevitably replace a constant feeling of intimacy and union by a feeling of separation. They deprive a husband of one of the great enjoyments of daily life—to go to sleep with the loved one in his arms; to awaken in the night or at daybreak and feel her at his side. And they deprive a wife of the corresponding enjoyment.

The double bed, on the other hand, promotes reconciliations. After the occasional quarrels which are inseparable from daily life, it is easy to go to sleep in separate beds and sulk. When husband and wife lie side by side, it is much easier, almost inevitable, to kiss and make up. The common bed promotes those little intimacies, those happy talks, that lead imperceptibly to slumber; and from the outset it should be a rule to keep that period for such talks, deferring all unpleasant discussions to some other time.

While a study [108] in California found no average difference in happiness between couples who occupied one bed and those who slept in two, yet observation shows that in many instances the move from the double bed to twin beds, later perhaps to separate rooms, is merely the symptom of a break in the harmony of the marriage, which is a prelude to its destruction. The average bride and groom, picking out furniture, are too much at the mercy of the salesman. When he says, "Twin beds, of course?" they have not the courage to face his scorn by a refusal; particularly if he follows up his advantage by insisting, "We don't sell many double beds any more; they're out of style."

If two beds are occupied, intelligent partners make it a rule to retire together in one, separating before they fall asleep, or occasionally spending the night together. This helps to prevent the growth—so fatally easy—of the feeling I have mentioned, that the husband seeks his wife only when he wants intercourse, and consequently the feeling on her part that he is more interested in her sexuality than in her personality. But even used in this way, the twin bed is less convenient as well as more expensive. Scientifically, my judgment is that healthy young couples should keep the double bed. Leave twin beds to the twins.

Don't Start at Too High
or Too Low a Level.

Returning from the honeymoon, husband and wife generally prepare to "settle down." Do not think of it! Marriage is not a process of settling down, nor a rut to be settled into. The minute a marriage settles down, it has lost much of its value. If you want to settle down, do so in the cemetery, so your heirs will not be put to the extra expense of moving the corpses later. As long as husband and wife are really living, they will not settle down; they will not make the mistake of thinking that matrimony is a static affair. It is not static but dynamic: it is a continuous interplay of two continually changing personalities, each of which is constantly changing the other and in turn being changed by the other; and thus the two go on indefinitely, life each year being richer, more exciting, and more enjoyable, as well as more complicated.

If the marriage is to follow this desirable pattern, it must not start off at so high a level that there is no place for it to go except down. Let me make this clearer by an illustration. Bert thought that Julia was simply wonderful. Nothing could be too good for her; he could not possibly do enough for her; she was a goddess to be adored and waited upon. They spent their honeymoon in his cabin in the mountains. He insisted on doing all the cooking and housework—she had nothing to do but sit around and be worshiped. They came back in a couple of weeks to a little apartment, and he continued this policy. He prepared breakfast, which he brought to her in bed. She did not dress until well into the middle of the morning, after he had gone to work. He came home at night as early as he could and got most of the dinner for her as well; after dinner he usually washed the dishes, she favoring him with her society and perhaps giving a little perfunctory help. On Sundays he frequently spent a large part of the day housecleaning—anything to serve her, to protect her from dirt and effort, to allow her to devote her time to the finer things of life, to enjoy herself.

And he succeeded! This was almost too good to be true; but Julia had been educated for marriage in the Romantic School anyhow, and she decided that luck was with her—she had found a perfect husband. The more he did for her, the more she took it for granted. Marriage was like that.

In a few months the pace began to tell. Not only did Bert begin to weary, just the least bit, in well-doing, but the boss began to suggest pointedly that unless he could arrive earlier and stay later at the office, and unless he could devote some of his evenings to his own advancement, his future was dark. Bert became panicky and swung to the other extreme. He explained to Julia, frankly and in what he thought was a straightforward and business-like way, that it would be for the benefit of their marriage, and consequently for her benefit, if she began to wait on him, to let him have his free time for his work.

The castle came down around Julia's head. Here they

were, not yet married a hundred days, and Bert's love had already cooled. He cared more for his work than he did for his bride! He went through months of difficulty, involving a couple of brief pilgrimages "back to mother" on the part of Julia, before they finally adjusted their marriage to the status of a co-operative partnership instead of a mere incense-burning institution.

Bert had started something that he could not finish.

The ordinary process of settling down is marked by the beginning of friction, sometimes with violent and unreasonable quarrels. The honeymoon is over when the couple stop saying to each other, "Darling, you're absolutely perfect!" and start saying to each other, "The trouble with you is—!" This change is brought about by many factors, of which three are particularly prominent:

1. *The greater intimacy of husband and wife,* which leads to greater emotional tension.

2. *The increased number of subjects with which they deal,* the broadening of their areas of contact. They might previously have agreed on almost everything; but new problems, new responsibilities, new acquaintances, new occupations now appear; and they need not be surprised to find that in some of these unforeseen situations they disagree.

3. *The gradual passing of some of the glamour.* People differ enormously in this respect, but there is no doubt that a great many live in a sort of dream world before marriage. Neither really sees the other: each sees an imaginary person to whom the partner's name is

given. The gradual descent to reality through this dis-illusionment has been extremely painful for some people, and emphasizes the importance of going into marriage without any more self-hypnotizing than is really necessary!

Marriage need not be built upon illusion, but it need not be built upon disillusionment either. Those who swing to the other extreme, after entering marriage in a state of emotional intoxication, are not managing their affairs with common sense. Of course you have seen your wife at her best in the past. Why not continue to do so? Why begin to ignore all the virtues which you formerly, and correctly, recognized, and begin to see only her defects? Of course she has some defects, just as have you and every other human being. It is for you to decide whether you are going to concentrate on these, or on the virtues which are still there and which are, in fact, probably increasing; which certainly will increase if you manage the marriage intelligently.

This matter of so-called disillusionment is really just the old story of the doughnut and the hole in another setting. The success and enjoyment of the marriage will depend largely upon whether you consciously and deliberately keep its good points in sight during the next forty years, or whether you consciously and deliberately begin to ignore these and look for trouble.

If you have planned your married life during the betrothal period, you will be prepared from the outset to meet the various new problems that now arise: the budget, the matter of recreation, the relationships with various members of the family on both sides, and so on. No particular rules need be or can be given. Marriages are not run successfully on rules. They are guided successfully, just as an automobile is guided successfully, by knowing where you are going and keeping your eye on the road.

Suppose you asked me how to get from the office of the American Institute of Family Relations down to the beach. I would not say, "Turn your steering wheel 14° to the right, keep it in that position for 34 seconds, then turn 18° to the left; after 82 seconds turn 90° to the left," and so on. You would have run into an electric-light pole long before you reached the first turn. All that is necessary is for me to give you a map, point out your destination, and tell you to take any good road that leads in that direction, meanwhile keeping your eye on the road.

Marriage is little different. If you head toward the goal of successfully founding a family that will yield the fullest and richest experience of life to yourself, your wife, and your offspring, if you keep your eye on that goal and take any turn that is necessary to carry you toward that goal, you will reach it in normal running time—and you will have a grand trip.

Chapter XVIII

CHILDREN

PHILOSOPHERS have filled libraries with contradictory treatises on "the meaning of life." I do not propose to compete with them, but from a biological point of view there are two principal motives for existence. The individual is interested in a full and harmonious functioning of all his capabilities; the species is interested in the production of children. Since the individual can not live fully without children, the interests of the two coincide. There is, therefore, biologically speaking, no more satisfactory goal than the production and rearing of sound children.

From their offspring, parents derive great advantages that they can get *in no other way*.

Normal human beings do not have to be urged to have children, any more than they have to be urged to marry. Nevertheless, an examination of some of the reasons why offspring fill the place that they do in the human heart will make for clear thinking.[37] In addition to the satisfaction of whatever primitive instincts may be bound up with childbearing, progeny are valued for such reasons as the following:

1. *They give a unique experience and education to the parents.* It is impossible to appreciate the nature and

extent of this at second hand; it must be felt. Man's personality and character (as well as woman's) is an incomplete—hopelessly and pathetically incomplete—thing unless it has included the joys—and occasional sorrows—of bringing up a family. "Some, indeed," says John M. Cooper, "break under the test and training, but they are the exceptions. How frequently, in the case of newly married couples, particularly after the birth of their first child, do we see the vital change that comes over both husband and wife—a putting away of the trivial and weakly sentimental, a deepening and enriching of the finer sentiments, a sobering sense of marital and parental responsibility, a flowering of unselfishness. Under the magic of family responsibility, even the painted doll often grows into a woman, and the callow stripling into a man."

2. *They bind the parents together.* Not only do husband and wife, separately, benefit from their children, but their community life is enriched and deepened as is possible in no other way. Marriage is successful to the extent that it is a genuine sharing, a co-operation in a joint enterprise. What can a husband and wife share more completely, deeply, and permanently, than their own children? Hence it is no coincidence that happily married couples have more children than do the unhappy, and that there is a regular association between size of family and happiness in marriage; while among the divorcees one finds that a majority never had any children and the rest average only one child apiece (see Appendix VII).

3. *They bring rejuvenation.* Watching the development of his child, sharing its experiences, its pleasures and pains, the parent lives over again, in memory and imagination, his own boyhood. This process is normally repeated a second time, with the grandchildren. The best way to remain young is to live with children.

4. *They give love in old age.* One of the saddest things in life—so say those who are old enough to know—is to see one's friends gradually passing away, leaving one isolated with none to care. This progressive bereavement, which casts a shadow over one's declining years, is diminished by a family of children whose love and comradeship are dependable as long as life endures.

5. *They give assistance in old age.* No one anticipates being supported by his children in the future; nevertheless, it is impossible to foresee the revolutions of the wheel of fortune, and those who have healthy and capable progeny need not fear to be left alone, impoverished and friendless, as a public charge.

6. *They confer immortality*—potentially at least. As to the continuation of personal existence after death, no one knows; it is a question of belief, and each is entitled to believe what he finds most plausible and comforting. The only immortality of which one can speak with confidence is that derived from the continuation of the chain of life through offspring. One's children are literally a part of one; they carry on the same existence that their ancestors enjoyed, without a break, clear back to the beginning of life on the globe. A man actually lives on, in his posterity, and has a right to feel

that he himself is thus projected ahead, to exercise his own personal influence on the world in each generation, to work and love in constantly renewed and slightly changing reincarnation.[97]

To the man capable of sentiment, this terrestrial immortality is a very real thing; and it is a correspondingly gloomy reflection that the birth-rate has fallen so low in the United States at present that the probability [112] is less than one in eight that the male descendants of any new-born infant will continue to perpetuate his family name.

The Machine Age Disregards Most
of the Needs of Children.

Children being thus valuable, their welfare is of first importance. It is surprising, therefore that there has grown up in the United States such a reluctance to face this fact. From a good deal of modern discussion one would think that children were a misfortune; that the smallest possible number was the desirable number; and that each additional child was for the mother a step toward the grave, for the father a step toward bankruptcy, and for both a step toward misery.

This idea is an easy outgrowth of the whole spirit of the Machine Age and its accompanying movement of population from the farms to the cities. On the farm the family is the unit; in the city the individual is the unit. Among individuals, the Machine Age is concerned only with the vigorous adult who is a maximum producer and who is preferably unencumbered—to use the familiar and really tragic term. The Machine Age has no interest in the old or the young. They must look out for themselves. Children being from its point of view merely an unprofitable nuisance, an economic liability, it makes little effort (except in a few sentimental ways) to promote their welfare. It does more for their health than formerly; it gives them longer formal schooling, but it takes no account of them in fixing the hours or places of work of their parents, or the pay of their parents.

These very real difficulties have been intensified by an emotional propaganda, much of which was associated with the earlier years of the birth-control movement.[59] For well on to a quarter of a century, America was assailed with propaganda painting the evils of large families, the dangers of childbearing, the misfortunes of the "unwanted child" (without taking much trouble to inquire *why* he was unwanted). To say that this birth-control propaganda was well intentioned and was sponsored by many admirable men and women, does not in the least diminish the harm that it did. It is only within the last few years that the official birth-control movement, both in the United States and in Great Britain, has begun to get its balance, to admit that many families should have fewer children and many others more children.

With all these adverse influences, it is not surprising that the birth-rate in the United States has fallen to the point where no longer are enough children being born to take the places of the people who die. Of all women who marry, in the white population of the United States, one fourth will never produce a child.[125] Some die, some are widowed, some divorced; while more than 18 per cent of all wives who survive in unbroken marriages are permanently childless; and if one takes only the educated classes, the percentage of permanently child-less marriages is still higher, and the majority of these voluntarily so—they have no children, because they de-liberately decided not to have children.[86]

While one fourth of all wives produce no children, one fifth produce a child apiece, another fifth two children apiece. This leaves, roughly speaking, one third of all white wives producing more or less normal fam-ilies, since three or more children per married couple are necessary to keep the race from dying out.

Under these circumstances, the normal family be-comes more than ever an evidence of superiority. The fathers who have such families are the most successful men,[131] the mothers the healthiest and longest-lived women.

So much emotional propaganda has created the oppo-site impression, that it is worth while to underline these facts. The man who gets along best in his profession, who rises to the top, who enjoys the most prestige and the largest salary is not, as one might suppose, the bach-elor with no encumbrances, or the childless man whose wife has nothing to do except to help him. The most successful men in any particular group are the ones with the most children;[128] the least successful have fewer children; until one gets down to the relative failures, the men who have not lived up to the expectations of themselves or their friends in business or profession: they include a disproportionate number of childless men and bachelors.[36]

Similarly, within any ordinary group, it is the woman with the largest family who lives longest, not the childless or unmarried woman.[51] Pregnancy is a normal state, and one not to be feared but rather looked forward to with the keenest anticipation.* Many women find that their enjoyment of life and their sense of well-being are greater during pregnancy than at any other time. Indeed, it occasionally restores a woman to health, and definitely cures some disabilities. The woman who frets, fumes, and makes herself miserable during pregnancy is often merely the neurotic woman. Oswald Spengler remarked that the modern woman has neuroses instead of babies. Some women, however, have both.

Usually a young couple want to delay the first pregnancy for at least a short time after marriage.[5] If the bride is in her thirties and her natural fertility is declining steadily, delay may be inadvisable; but for the younger woman there is often good reason to take the first year after marriage to become adjusted to the new status of wife, before beginning adjustment to still another status, that of mother. But it is sometimes fatally

---

* Much has been said of the high death rate of women, associated with childbirth. This puerperal mortality has decreased in recent years, but it is important to recognize that at least one-third of it should not be credited to childbirth at all, since it is the result of abortion.

easy to keep putting off the first baby, with a resulting great injustice to all concerned, and particularly to the wife. The husband finds completion of his sexual life, from the merely physical point of view, in coitus; the wife's body, on the other hand, is made not merely for that function but for bearing children as well; and she is not leading a normal and wholesome life unless she has some pregnancies.

Sex of the Offspring Cannot be Controlled.

There is no known way of controlling the sex of the child, and the many schemes in circulation with that intent are fallacious. The fact [58] is that the sex of the offspring is determined primarily by the nature of the cells that unite, and this is a matter of chance. Women produce only one kind of egg-cell, which may for the sake of algebra be called X; men produce two kinds of spermatozoa, X and Y, in equal numbers. A single ejaculation may contain up to 500,000,000 spermatozoa, and only one of these can fertilize the egg-cell. The one that reaches it first is the one that determines the sex of the offspring. The combination XX will produce a female child, the combination XY a male. For all practical purposes it may be said that the sex of the child is as much a matter of chance as is throwing double sixes with a pair of dice, and that there is nothing the parents can do to affect it. However, the father can at least have the satisfaction of knowing that it is he who controls the sex of the offspring; the mother, who produces only one kind of egg-cell, has nothing to say about it. On the other hand, if you want a boy and get a girl, do not blame your wife—you are the one who is responsible!

If no preventive is employed, cases are numerous where a bride has conceived on her wedding night. More frequently, however, she will not conceive for some days, or weeks, or even months; and in some cases, never. These sterile marriages are in most instances tragedies; but a good deal can be done to prevent or even cure them. A proper pre-marital examination will eliminate many difficulties.

The sterility of the marriage may be due to either the husband or the wife. It is too easy to blame the latter; and good practice demands that the man be examined first, since it is a simple matter, by inspecting a condom specimen, to determine at least whether he is producing an ample number of active and apparently normal spermatozoa. The wife can then be examined. If her reproductive organs are apparently normal and her fallopian tubes open (as is easily determined by passing air through them), the difficulty may be constitutional. The level of fertility among civilized people is none too high anyhow, and in many instances both husband and wife are low enough in this respect to produce a sterile mating. Better balanced diet, exercise, sunshine, sleep, sometimes the administration of vitamins and hormones, may bring both up above the threshold, so that pregnancy ensues. Success cannot be guaranteed in all cases;

but if a pregnancy is desired and no signs of it appear within a year, lose no time in consulting some properly qualified specialist, if you can find one.

In cases of permanent and incurable sterility, adoption is the alternative. Unfortunately, the demand for children suitable for adoption is much greater than the supply; but it is often possible to find a child who deserves the home you can give; and in a majority of instances the experiment will turn out successfully.[67] Better still, in a surprisingly large number of cases the adoption of a child is followed by the wife's own pregnancy.[48] Apparently the lessened tension, the more favorable emotional states, produced by the presence of a baby in the home are sufficient to change her own body chemistry, and perhaps that of her husband, so markedly as to remove the sterility. It is merely another illustration of the importance of children in the life of the individual. Figuratively speaking, it would not be too much to say that the bachelor is only one third alive. After he marries, he is two thirds alive; when he becomes a father, he is really and completely living.

The first pregnancy will run its course in its appointed way; and as there are so many books dealing with this subject, I shall not touch on it here. An occasional woman behaving as if it were a calamity or a punishment exploits it to get undeserved sympathy; and some husbands are so self-centered and childish that they resent pregnancy as tending to deprive them of the wife's entire attention; but with the ordinary couple the course of the pregnancy brings them steadily closer together, deepening and enriching their common life. It is now well understood that the mother cannot "mark" or influence the development of the baby in any particular way.[50] Its development is determined by the inherited potentialities contained in the original egg and sperm cells. Its development is favored in a general—not in any specific—way if the mother is healthy and happy; and it is the duty of the father to keep her so.

Next to his own considerate attention, one of the things he can do is to help her keep out of the wrong kind of company. There are unfortunately some women who take delight in discovering a girl in her first pregnancy and filling her up with hair-raising stories of their own symptoms and sufferings, or those of someone else they know, under similar conditions. This may gratify their own desire to feel important, but it is sometimes disastrous to the sensitive mind of an inexperienced young bride. Wholesome girls about her own age, who already have children, are the most suitable companions, and the ones to whom she turns naturally.

Childbirth Should Be Regarded as a Wholly Normal Function.

With such influences, she should approach the experience of childbirth as a normal biological function rather than a terrifying ordeal. Her pain in childbirth will depend to some extent on her own attitude, unconscious as well as conscious. It can hardly be denied that this experience has been magnified by some women into a

terrifying thing, because of their own neurotic personalities. The neuroses are not confined to the women,
however; many a husband is just as silly, or even tries
to go his wife one better by exaggerating her sufferings
and asserting that if it depended on him to bear babies
there would be no further population of the world—he
could never face it, etc., etc., etc. I have known a number of instances in which a marriage was childless because the husband, not the wife, professed to dread the
terrors of childbirth so much! Unquestionably the husband cannot understand what his wife faces, in any
complete sense, because he can never have the first-hand
experience. So that he may get at least a correct description of one case, I have added in Appendix VII a
case history; it is presented merely as a description, not
necessarily typical of all cases, for of course no two
women react in just the same way to the situation.

When a man ventures to comment on the pains of
childbirth, he at once exposes himself to the obvious retort from all women, that he does not know what he is
talking about. Accepting this rebuke in advance, and
speaking only as man to man, I would merely remark
that the various hazards, distresses, and tortures that
women undergo in childbirth are certainly not more
serious than the various hazards, distresses, and tortures
which men undergo in war; with the difference that,
after it is all over, women have something worth while
to show for it.

A normal family,[59] in a home that can give children
a favorable start in life, consists of four or more chil-

dren; and it is desirable that these children be spaced far enough apart to give the mother every opportunity to do justice to each one as well as to herself. Nature has taken care of this to some extent by making it a little less likely that the mother will conceive while she is nursing a child. If she nurses the baby for eight or ten months, it will be seen that, even without any precautions, children would not naturally follow one another at intervals of less than about two years. This can be verified in any old genealogy, going back to the pioneer days when larger families were the rule, and contraceptive measures less used. It is quite usual to note that the children came along pretty regularly every two years.

The rule of non-conception during lactation, like most other rules concerning the human sexual life, is variable, however. Some women will conceive at almost any time. A new pregnancy usually involves weaning the nursling so that the mother will not have to tax her strength by feeding two babies from her body at once. This is an injustice to the baby at the breast, since no food can fully take the place of mother's milk. It is also a great injustice psychologically to mother and child, since the emotional satisfaction and emotional development of both is promoted by the process of nursing at the breast. The moral is that the husband must prevent his wife from becoming pregnant while she is nursing a baby. She should wait until the baby is weaned; and many mothers want some months of rest after that, before beginning the next pregnancy. This plan will bring the babies about three years apart, giving the mother a chance meanwhile to participate in normal social life.

It is possible to make the family cover a much longer period of time: to space the babies four, five, or six years apart. This has many disadvantages that counterbalance such real or imaginary advantages as may be attributed to it. It is a drawback to the children to be of such unequal age, for they are not such good playmates for each other. The alternative plan favored by many parents is to have the babies come in pairs: two children fairly close together; then a delay until they are able to run about and take some care of themselves, thereby demanding less of the mother's time and energy; then two more. Most parents theorize that it would be a great convenience to have triplets or quadruplets and "get it over with"; but few are able to apply this theory in practice.

Every argument urges parents to begin their family early, complete it early, and have the rest of their lives to enjoy it and themselves, with abundant time for outside interests. Of course this involves giving up some other things, but in the long run it is a good investment. History is filled with the remarks of famous men who at the close of lives of tremendous activity and attainment spoke bitterly of the hollowness and futility of the whole thing, agreeing with The Preacher that "All is vanity." I cannot recall ever hearing of a parent who, after successfully bringing up a worthy family, on looking back over this achievement expressed any regret over a misspent life.

APPENDICES

APPENDIX I

THE FEMININITY AND HAPPINESS OF WIVES

| | FEMININITY | | | |
	HIGH	AVERAGE	Low	TOTALS
Happy	376	485	130	991=67%
	69%	71%	51%	
Doubtful	71	99	46	216=15%
Unhappy	95	99	78	272=18%
	17%	14%	31%	
	542	683	254	1,479
	37%	46%	17%	

The differences between high and average femininity are not statistically significant, but the differences between average and low are important. In the happy group, the difference between low and average has a critical ratio of 4.4. (The critical ratio is the ratio between the observed difference of two percentages and the standard error of the difference.) In the unhappy group, the difference between average and low has a critical ratio of 6.3. Differences between low and high are equally significant: CR 4.0 in the happy group, 4.6 in the unhappy group.

HAPPINESS AND DURATION OF MARRIAGE

LENGTH OF MARRIAGE IN YEARS

	0–4	5–9	10–14	15–19	20–24	25 and up	TOTAL
Happy	416	283	299	185	140	146	1,469= 68%
	73%	61%	70%	70%	71%	72%	
Doubtful ...	75	100	73	38	34	30	350= 16%
Unhappy	82	82	66	40	23	26	319= 16%
Total	573	465	438	263	197	202	2,138=100%

When the happy and unhappy (omitting the doubt-fuls) are correlated with the duration of the marriage, bi-serial $r = .039 \pm .023$ and tetra-choric $r = .03$; in other words, there is no relation whatever between the duration of the marriage and its happiness. This corresponds with the findings of a smaller study [108] in which the length of the marriage correlated —.028 with the husband's happiness and —.048 with the wife's happiness.

The only break in the line is the interesting drop in happiness during the last half of the first decade. This was also found in the smaller study, where it was interpreted as "in part due to the waning of honeymoon happiness and in part to growing discord in certain marriages which will later be dissolved by divorce." This is offset by the fact that some marriages improve steadily, a period of early conflict being followed by the attainment of greater emotional maturity of both partners, with consequent greater understanding and contentment. The period six or eight years after marriage is the principal danger point, but wise planning will enable partners to avoid its difficulties easily.

THE MASCULINITY AND HAPPINESS OF HUSBANDS

	MASCULINITY			
	HIGH	AVERAGE	LOW	TOTALS
Happy	373	481	146	1,000= 66%
	67%	72%	54%	
Doubtful	75	101	54	230= 16%
Unhappy	109	84	70	263= 18%
	19%	13%	26%	
Total	557	666	270	1,493=100%
	36%	44%	20%	

The differences between the high and the average masculine do not carry much weight (CR in the happy group 1.6, in the unhappy group 2.4). When those who are low in masculinity are compared, however, they make a uniformly unfavorable showing. In the happy group, the low masculines are differentiated from the average (CR 4.5) and the high (CR 3.2) very distinctly; while the converse relationship is found in the unhappy group, between those with low and high masculinity (CR 2.8) and still more strikingly between those of low and average masculinity (CR 6.0).

ARE YOU THE PERFECT SON-IN-LAW?

Directions for scoring: After each of the following 10 questions you will find a set of five scoring figures, 0 1 2 3 4. Check the figure which represents your answer to each question on this basis:

0 means "not at all", "never."

1 means "somewhat", "sometimes", "a little."

2 means "an average amount", "about as often as not."

3 means "usually", "a good deal", "frequently."

4 means "entirely", "practically always."

1. You make the in-laws feel as much at home in your house as are the members of your own family.
   0 1 2 3 4

2. You get along without any financial help from your wife's family.   0 1 2 3 4

3. You make the in-laws feel that you like them, not because they are related to your wife, but because they are wonderful people.   0 1 2 3 4

4. You show a friendly tolerance toward all the views of the in-laws.   0 1 2 3 4

5. You are prepared to be helpful in any possible way in case of trouble in your wife's family.   0 1 2 3 4

6. You attend strictly to your own affairs in case fric-

tion arises between your wife and any of the members of her own family. 0 1 2 3 4

7. You include the in-laws in appropriate social affairs that would particularly interest them or be of value to them. 0 0 2 3 4

8. You make your wife feel that one of the best things about your marriage is the relationship with her family which it brought you. 0 1 2 3 4

9. You radiate an atmosphere of happiness when you visit your wife's family. 0 1 2 3 4

10. You maintain control of your own home so tactfully that the in-laws scarcely recognize the fact that they have nothing whatever to say about it.

0 1 2 3 4

After each question, draw a ring around the number that describes you best. Add up these scores. If your score is 40, you are perfect; and you should go over the scale again, more carefully, and find out just where you failed to tell the truth. Probably few men can justly claim a score of more than 30. If you are very low on any item, take that as a cue to improve your behavior on that particular point.

Appendix V

Where

~~HOW~~ MEN PROPOSE

PLACE	REJECTED	ACCEPTED AND LATER BROKEN	FOLLOWED BY MARRIAGE	TOTALS
At her home	84	15	173	272 23%
Riding or driving	97	20	176	293 25%
Vacation, resort, train or ship	48	12	90	150 13%
By letter, telegram, or telephone	12	4	47	63 5%
Private party, dinner, or dance	45	7	71	123 10%
Street, park, restaurant, or other public place	92	12	138	242 20%
Miscellaneous	7	2	29	38 4%
	385 33%	72 6%	724 61%	1,181 100%

HAPPINESS OF MARRIAGE IN RELATION TO NUMBER OF CHILDREN

NUMBER OF CHILDREN

	0	1	2	3	4	5 AND UP	TOTAL
Happy	1,063	1,196	1,351	778	546	569	5,503 = 66%
Doubtful ...	135	153	151	110	64	71	684 = 8%
Unhappy	590	583	478	242	108	182	2,183 = 26%
Totals	1,788	1,932	1,980	1,130	718	822	8,370 = 100%

The happy couples average 2.04 children each, the unhappy ones 1.67 children each. Of the childless couples 59 per cent are happy in marriage, of the couples with three or more children, 71 per cent are happy in marriage, a highly reliable difference with CR 12. It must be remembered that these are all completed marriages, none being included unless it was certain, because of the wife's age or other reason, that no more children would be born. Hence a large part of the childless couples had presumably been subtracted through the divorce court. Omitting the doubtfuls, happiness of marriage was correlated with the number of children, giving bi-serial $r = .15 \pm .01$ and tetrachoric r (those with no children or only one, against all the rest) $= .19$. All these marriages were in the educated part of the population.

Appendix VII

MY FIRST BABY
By M. W.

For nine months I had carried my baby, and he had become, oh, so heavy. My body felt as if it were dead. Neither standing, sitting, nor lying down could I be wholly comfortable; only at work could I forget momentarily the pressure in my abdomen.

On Monday I had prepared lunch for some guests, and after it we were all in the patio, I sitting in the hammock, when the membranes surrounding my child broke—quite painlessly—and the fluid in which he had been floating began to escape. I went to my room and got into bed while father telephoned the doctor; but as I did not understand at that time just what had happened, I did not give intelligent information. The doctor said he was coming out in our neighborhood that afternoon and would see me between four and five o'clock.

Had he adhered to this decision there might have been lots of trouble, but as luck would have it he arrived about two o'clock, before calling on his other patients, and at once recognized what had occurred. By this time, too, my labor pains had begun. I had long wondered what they would feel like, and whether I would be able to recognize them as anything different from the various pains I had enjoyed for several months. I found, as had been predicted, that they are unmistakable, and the term "bearing down pains" well describes them. But they were at first not so very different from pains frequently felt during menstruation.

While father telegraphed to John, my husband, who was on our ranch in New Mexico, 200 miles away—for my delivery had not been expected for a fortnight longer—I made ready to start for the hospital in El Paso. Over my kimono I put the all-enveloping cape which I had worn in public for several months, and sat with father in the rear seat of the doctor's car. That was a wild ride! We violated all the speed laws, and passed traffic policemen with no consideration for their feelings, but I never expect to cover four longer miles than those. I was in misery, and sat with my legs stiffened out, groaning and calling to the doctor, and looking ahead for car tracks and other bumps that particularly tortured me. Although the day was warm, my feet and legs were ice cold. My pains were coming with intervals of only two or three minutes between, and as I described them to the doctor, it was made evident that we had no time to waste. By the time we had come down from the Mesa, he decided it would not be safe to try to reach the hospital for which we had started. Another was on our route, and we turned in there. I was assisted into a wheel chair, pushed over the bumps of what seemed to be an interminable number of thresholds into an elevator and rolled directly into the delivery room. It was about half-past four.

For months—indeed, for years—I had lived in imagination the time of the coming of my first baby, and wondered what my sensations would be; wondered how I would stand it; wondered whether I would be able to know everything that went on, or whether I would lose consciousness; wondered if I would come through it alive. Now that I was on the threshold of the great experience, my principal feeling was one of excitement—apart, of course, from the pains, which, coming only a minute apart, were almost continuous. I was a little bewildered by the breathless speed of the whole performance, for I had been led to suppose that I would have twenty-four hours or more from the beginning of labor pains to the appearance of my child.

But I was glad, for I had determined in my own mind weeks before—though this determination doubtless had little to do with the results—that I would get it over with as soon as possible. And now my body was being racked by the expulsive pains that showed my time had come.

They were the worst thing I had ever experienced; I thought at the moment that they could not be worse. I had not imagined that they would be so painful. The accounts which my married friends had poured out on me were vague and unintelligible, even though sometimes harrowing. So I knew almost nothing about what I was to expect; except that I had looked for a long, exhausting process, and now, in the short space of time required to bring me to the hospital, it seemed to be reaching its culmination. My excitement was almost intoxicating, although I felt desperate, helpless, to think that John was not with me to share in the experience I was about to undergo.

It took but a minute for us to reach the delivery room, and little longer for me to be undressed, lifted on the table, swathed in a hideous gown, shaved, painted with iodine, and given lots of miscellaneous encouragement from the bystanders, who irritated me exceedingly. I wished that they would mind their own business and let me attend to mine. There was one little nurse who seemed to be unused to such experiences, and who looked badly frightened. The doctor had told her to wash her hands for ten minutes—if my understanding was correct—and I can never forget the picture she made standing there, trembling, apparently ready to cry, and alternately soaping and rinsing her hands for what seemed to be a whole afternoon. She was swallowing hard, and stiffening her neck and mouth, as if she were trying to keep from showing distress. Another nurse looked so cold and indifferent that I immediately hated her. A third seemed to be chewing gum. I despised them all, and wanted no one around except the doctor. I felt that he was the only person who could really do anything for me, and at each recurrence of pain I longed to have him near me. I tried to shut my mind to what I considered the impertinent and useless chatter of the nurses, who were doing their best to encourage me by telling me how brave I was. I did not feel brave—merely desperate, and determined to get the business over with as soon as possible. I thought if I totally ignored them—snubbed them, so to speak—they would perhaps leave me alone and let me work out my own problem, my life problem. My feet were put on foot-rests; straps on which to pull were placed in my hands; and I settled down to the job of getting my child into the world. I had but one will: to release him as rapidly as possible. Yet my concentration on this painful task did not prevent my mind from working incessantly on all sorts of related subjects. I pictured John driving furiously down the valley, and was inclined to be angry because he had not been with me at the time. Then I thought how disappointed he would be to miss all the excitement I was having. It transpired later that at the hour his son and heir was born, he was sitting in the dust repairing a tire.

While a part of my mind was thus engaged outside my body, another part was directing all my energies into my muscles. I stiffened my legs until I raised my body entirely above the table, and had to be pushed back down on it by the doctor. I pulled and pulled on those straps until I thought they must break. I was at length rewarded by feeling the head of my little baby enter the channel into the outer world.

I felt as if I were about to split open. This period remains in my mind today as the most intense of the whole experience. I sensed the channel being dilated wider and wider, and yet the child seemed to remain in one place, whereas I wanted to feel it moving toward the outer air. It was maddening.

The doctor approached with ether. I protested that I did not want to be anesthetized. I did not tell him why; but the reason was that I did not want to miss a single feature of this, the supreme experience of life. A woman's curiosity, you may say. Then, too, I feared that if I lost consciousness I would cease my own exertions, and therefore the baby would not be born so soon; and my dominant thought just then was to get him out into the world with as little delay as possible.

I was disposed to argue the matter; but the doctor told me ether was necessary to relax my muscles and make the birth easier and quicker, so I inhaled it in huge gasps. I felt myself slipping, then sinking down, down, softly and deliciously, as my arms and legs seemed to melt away, and then my trunk become reduced to a mere point. I rallied myself for one last mighty tug on the straps. A moment of panic seized me, as I wondered whether I would ever "come to"; I thought that perhaps I would never see my baby, after all. Then pain left me and I fell into a blissful unconsciousness.

In the ether I would hear the nurses' voices becoming louder and louder; then they would grow fainter and fainter as I again inhaled. The room would become indistinct, until I again lost consciousness and began to dream. Several times I dreamed that my baby had already been born. Other times I would dream that I was not in the hospital at all, but back in my home; then I would regain my senses, see the hospital room around me, and think that that was the real dream. When I emerged from the dreams I entered a world of smell—the odor of ether—and then saw the figure of the doctor looming up in the fog over me, unfamiliar in his white head-covering. I noted that he looked up frequently to the clock. The room seemed immensely high, and brought back to my mind similar sensations in childhood fevers.

Then I would feel the pain again—pains as if the contents of my abdomen were being torn out, together with stabbing pains, as if some one were rapidly running a knife into me in various directions. I have heard these described as "cutting and grinding pains," which is apt. During these pains I moaned or cried out, but I shed no tears.

Much of the time, it seemed like a nightmare rather than a real experience. As often as I thought of its reality, I thought of my mother, and then of all the women in the world who have given birth to babies, in the midst of suffering like mine. It gave me a new feeling toward womankind in general, as well as toward my own mother. "How hard life is!" I thought to myself; and I resolved that I would never bear another child.

Once I called out, "O God!" Then I reflected, "How funny that must sound to the nurses!" and I laughed a little to think that I had said it.

A phrase which my mother had once used flashed into my mind; "Pressing out the little life," she had said. That was just it. I repeated the expression over and over to myself, as I pressed. But my child seemed to make no progress toward the new world before him. Instead, he seemed to become humped up in one side of my body, so that part of my abdomen felt almost flat to my touch, while the other half was much distended.

At one time I heard an infant crying in the adjoining room, which is the nursery.

The next thing I knew the doctor was warning me to stop moving my legs, because the baby was between them.

Another flash; I saw the doctor holding a pair of scissors over me. I asked anxiously if he intended to cut me, and he replied that he did not. If my mind had been a little less disordered I would of course have known that the scissors were to sever the child's umbilical cord.

Another relapse into the ether. When I emerged I heard the doctor exclaim, "It's a boy!" My heart leaped, for I had wanted a boy, but to prevent disappointment I had almost persuaded myself that the first-born would be a girl.

Somewhere in this period I accidentally put my hand on my abdomen and felt it flat. Scarcely anything in the whole experience of the afternoon made a deeper impression on me than that. For so many weeks my abdomen had been enlarged, and now it was flat—or at least felt so to me. It made me realize keenly that my baby had left the maternal nest; that I was an actual mother and no longer "an expectant mother."

My consciousness of my surroundings began to be more sustained, although still foggy. I saw my baby held up in the air. I was shocked to see how large he was (as a fact, he weighed only six and one-fourth pounds) and wondered how there had ever been room for him in my small body. My vivid impression was that he was red with white streaks—the latter composed of the cheesy covering found on all new-born babies, which had not yet been wholly removed from him. He was not an object of beauty just then. I called out to him weakly, "O Juanito, you're ugly, but I love you." Then I again succumbed to the ether.

In my next period of consciousness the doctor instructed me to pull and bear down some more, and the placenta was soon expelled. He assisted by manipulating my abdomen, and I was again struck to note how soft it was, as compared with its former distended condition, to which I had become so accustomed.

Because of the ether, I missed one experience which I coveted above almost all others—the first cry of the child. I did not hear him cry at all while he was in the delivery room. After he had been taken out I caught the thin, dismal wail and excitedly asked, "Is that my baby?" "Yes; he's crying," a nurse replied. I laughed with hysterical joy. I had been desirous that my baby should cry spontaneously as soon as his head was born—before even his shoulders issued from my body; and that he should not, a weakling, have to be slapped into breathing. I asked the doctor next day and learned that Juanito (the Spanish form of "little John") had behaved just as I had hoped.

One more brief period of unconsciousness, then the effects of the ether began to wear off and my excite-

ment returned in equal measure. I now wanted to talk
a steady stream to the previously despised nurses, or to
anyone else in earshot; to talk of my baby, of my husband, of myself. While I was thus volubly engaged I
was lifted off the table and wheeled back to my room,
which father had in the meanwhile engaged for me.

The feeling of relief was heavenly. My body felt
light as a feather. My back, which had long been under a strain, was so comfortable that I scarcely knew
it was there.

On this brief trip I wept for the first time, however
—hysterical tears—because John was not in the hall to
greet me, and to share so far as he might in the experience which, I felt, belonged to both of us. I passed
dear father, who had been waiting in the hall most of
the time, and who followed me to my room. Deliriously
laughing and crying alternately, longing to talk of my
experience with everybody I saw, I was in a few seconds landed in my bed. It was five o'clock. I had been
in the delivery room just twenty-five minutes. I was
delighted, really, to have the doctor tell me next day
that while my confinement (a "dry birth") had been
short, it had been relatively painful, not easy. I was
proud to think, and to have my husband know, that
I had been able to face a real ordeal, and to survive
without flinching. Naturally, this sort of pride would
not have led me to desire a more painful delivery; but
since it so happened, I wanted to make the most of it.

I felt weak, as I said, but not remarkably sore or in
pain, considering what I had been through. I did not

even feel the most soreness next day, but rather the day following, when both arms and legs showed the strain to which I had subjected them. It is the same way after a mountain climb; one does not feel the stiffness so much on the day after as on the second day. In about forty-eight hours the stiffness in my arms began to bear testimony to the vigor with which I had pulled on those straps. My legs, although stiff, were less so than my arms.

My anxiety now was to know when John would come; I felt sure he would not be admitted to see me that night, and such proved to be the case. He arrived about eleven o'clock, but could not get in until next morning. I lay limply on the bed all night, scarcely sleeping at all; still living on the excitement of the event, and letting my mind run over and over it. I began to think that maybe some day I would bear another child; but not too soon.

At six o'clock the following morning Juanito was brought to me for the first time, and I devoured him with greedy eyes. He looked like his father—there was no doubt of it. I noted a hundred little traits, enumeration of which would be tedious to anyone but his parents. Most of all, I was pleased to note his typically masculine appearance—he was one hundred per cent boy and not the most unsophisticated old bachelor visitor could ever mistake him for anything else. I did not want a "sissy", and Juanito promised to live up to my ideal. Indeed, from the first day he displayed such marked characteristics of western manhood that the nurses in the hospital soon nicknamed him "Wild Bill."

I gave him the breast, which was supplied only with colostrum, my milk not appearing until twenty-four hours later. I have read of some woman who said that the most ecstatic joy she experienced in her entire lifetime was the moment when she felt her child first nursing at her breast. The sensation made no such overwhelming impression on me—it was interesting, and somewhat painful. Beyond that, it was slightly repugnant to me, mainly, no doubt, because of the pain associated with it—pain which ran clear through my abdomen. After a few days, as the pain disappeared, my repugnance to nursing abated, and I now enjoy the function.

My alarm was aroused by a big piece of surgeon's plaster gummed entirely around Juanito's little leg. I thought immediately of the scissors I had seen in the doctor's hand, and wondered what he had done to my boy. Closer observation would have shown me what I had to be told—that the strip of tape bore the number of my room, and was merely the child's identification tag.

A few hours later John came in, and thereafter spent almost the whole of every day with me, during the two weeks I remained in the hospital. I had many callers; four days after Juanito's birth I celebrated my own twenty-first birthday with quite a party, which brought its own ice cream. I am sure the hospital authorities were scandalized by the number of visitors I had, coming at all hours of the day. But even with this, my stay in the institution was most wearisome.

Moreover, the experiences of other newly-made mothers along the hall were distressing. Scarcely a day passed that I did not hear the moans and screams of some woman in childbirth, and my own nerves were not yet strong enough to receive them with equanimity. Perhaps in a maternity hospital, built especially for the purpose, a more successful effort is made to deaden the sounds; but in this one I was obliged to endure altogether too much of the suffering of other women, in addition to my own little share.

As the baby was brought to me only at the three-hour intervals required for alimentation, he did not seem to be really mine; I felt no actual sense of ownership. Moreover, I was scared of my responsibility whenever he was beside me. And now that I am at home with him, where he is under my eyes almost all the time, I cannot yet realize that I am actually a mother. It still seems like a dream. No doubt the feeling of possession will grow on me. It was the same with marriage—I did not feel myself to be radically a different person during the month after the wedding than during the month before; in fact, it took a year or more for me to become adjusted to the feeling that my status had changed, and that I was a different person. I suppose it will be the same with motherhood. Anyhow, Juanito is growing sweeter every day. He is twenty-one days old this afternoon—his twenty-first birthday, one might say.

I am beginning to get over my awe of him. At first, as I said, I was frightened by my own offspring, in spite of the fact that I have been familiar with babies all my life, having helped bring up my own brothers and sisters and numerous progeny of other people. But Juanito seemed so little, and fragile, that I scarcely dared touch him; indeed, while I caressed him tenderly, I am sure that he was at least a week old before I dared to kiss him for the first time. When we brought him home, at the end of our fortnight in the hospital, and I had for the first time the responsibility of him day and night, I was almost paralyzed with fear. The first bath I gave him was a delicate operation, indeed. Now I have learned what a tough, wiry, vigorous little fellow he is, and I am only delighted, not terrified, by him.

I am quite sure that this lying-in period—an appropriate name!—has been more trying to me than my pregnancy. Although I had some physical discomfort, often marked distress, yet I was able to keep busy then, and to be as active as I desired. Now, on the contrary, while I feel just as restless and mentally full of energy as ever, my ability to do what I want to do is limited. I long to clean house, to wash Juanito's diapers, to do all sorts of drudgery, as well as many things that are considered more esthetic. I did not feel such inescapable restlessness before. Indeed, during the later months of my pregnancy I enjoyed a feeling of tranquillity greater than at any other period of my life. When I met people I felt more superiority and self-possession; now, I have returned temporarily to the nervous eagerness of my premarital days.

But in a few weeks more I know that this will disappear. Life is becoming more wonderful each day, as Juanito and I each gain strength. I can hardly wait for that most interesting period of all, when a baby begins to sit up, to walk, and to talk. I have much to look forward to; yet much also on which I can look back with joy. I have no feeling of reluctance to entering on another pregnancy, in due time; for Juanito must have brothers and a sister. Of course, the thrill of the event can never again be that which the birth of my first baby brought. That is a remembrance—even though already a somewhat dream-like remembrance—which is priceless. I can say truthfully that the experience of childbirth is, to me, so thrilling that I would gladly go through it—once—merely for the sake of the experience —even if I knew that I would not have a child of my own as the result of it. Think, then, what it means to me, when I have Juanito as well!

Appendix VIII

REFERENCES

1. Alvarez, Walter C. "Blood pressure in women as influenced by the sexual organs." Archives of Internal Medicine 37:597-626. May 15, 1926.
2. Angell, Robert Cooley. A study in undergraduate adjustment. Chicago, 1930.
3. ————. The family encounters the depression. New York, 1936.
4. Baber, Ray Erwin. Marriage and the family. New York, 1939.
5. Bernard, William S. "Student attitudes on marriage and the family." American Sociological Review 3(3):354-361. June, 1938.
6. Blanchard, Phyllis, and Carlyn Manasses. New girls for old. New York, 1930.
7. Bolin, J. S., and S. J. Holmes. "Marriage selection and scholarship." Journal of Heredity 18(6):253-256. June, 1927.
8. Bossard, James H. S. "Residential propinquity as a factor in marriage selection." American Journal of Sociology 38(2):219-224. Sept., 1932.
9. ————. "The age factor in marriage." American Journal of Sociology 38(4):536-547. Jan., 1933.
10. Bromley, Dorothy Dunbar, and Florence H. Britten. Youth and sex. New York, 1938.
11. Burgess, Ernest W., and Leonard S. Cottrell, jr. Predicting success or failure in marriage. New York, 1939.

12. Cahen, Alfred. Statistical analysis of American divorce. New York, 1932.

13. Carlson, J. Spencer, Stuart W. Cook, and Eleroy L. Stromberg. "Sex differences in conversation." Journal of Applied Psychology 20(6):727-735. Dec., 1936.

14. Cavan, Ruth Shonle, and Katherine H. Ranck. The family and the depression: a study of 100 Chicago families. Chicago, 1938.

15. Ciocco, Antonio. "On human social biology, III, Elements affecting the formation of the marital group." Human Biology 11 (2):234-247. May, 1939.

16. Conklin, Edmund S., Melba E. Byrom, and Alta Knips. "Some mental effects of menstruation." Pedagogical Seminary 34(3):357-367. Sept., 1927.

17. Davis, Katherine Bement. Factors in the sex life of 2200 women. New York, 1929.

18. Dickinson, Robert L., and Lura Beam. A thousand marriages: a medical study of sex adjustment. Baltimore, 1931.

19. Dudycha, G. J. "Sex differences in punctuality." Journal of Social Psychology 8:355-363. 1937.

20. Duncan, Otis D., J. H. McClure, J. Salisbury, and R. H. Simmons. "The factor of age in marriage." American Journal of Sociology 39:469-482. 1933.

21. Fenlason, Anne F., and A. R. Hertz. "The college student and feelings of inferiority." Mental Hygiene 22(3):389-399. July, 1938.

22. Fifteenth census of the U.S.:1930. Population: Marital condition. Washington, 1933.

23. Fiske, George Walter. The changing family. New York, 1928.

24. Folsom, Joseph Kirk. The family. New York, 1934.

25. Gosney, E. S., and Paul Popenoe. Sterilization for human betterment. New York, 1929.

26. Groves, Ernest Rutherford, and William Fielding Ogburn.

American marriage and family relationships. New York, 1928.

27. Hall, Fred S., and Mary E. Richmond. Child marriages in the U.S. New York, 1925.

28. Halle, Rita S. "Marriages made in college." Good Housekeeping 92(4):26 ff. April, 1931.

29. Hamilton, Gilbert V. A research in marriage. New York, 1929.

30. Hanson, Frank Blair. "The Pratt family: a record of human inbreeding for eight generations." Journal of Heredity 15(5):207-209. May, 1924.

31. Harris, John W. "Pregnancy and labor in young primiparae." Bulletin of Johns Hopkins Hospital 33:12-16. Jan., 1922.

32. Hart, Hornell, and Ella B. Personality and the family. Boston, 1935.

33. Harvey, O. L. "Some statistics derived from recent questionnaire studies relative to human sexual behavior." Journal of Social Psychology 3:161-188. 1932.

34. Harvey, P. N. "Notes on the relative mortality of married men and on an experiment in forecasting mortality over a limited period." Journal of the Institute of Actuaries 61(302):293-330. Dec., 1930.

35. Himes, Norman E. Practical birth control methods. New York, 1938.

36. Huntington, Ellsworth, and Leon F. Whitney. The builders of America. New York, 1927.

37. Johnson, Roswell H. "The motivation of childbearing." Eugenical News 12(11):(1-6). Nov., 1927.

38. Jones, Harold Ellis. "Homogamy in intellectual abilities." American Journal of Sociology 35(3):369-382. Nov., 1929.

39. Landis, Carney, and James D. Page. Modern society and mental disease. New York, 1938.

40. Lang, Richard O. A study of the degree of happiness or

unhappiness in marriage as rated by acquaintances of the married couples. Unpublished M. A. thesis, University of Chicago, 1932.

41. Lange, Johannes. "Die Folgen der Entmannung Erwachsener." Arbeit und Gesundheit, Heft 24. Leipzig, 1934.

42. Lehman, Harvey C., and Paul A. Witty. "Sex differences in vocational attitudes." Journal of Applied Psychology 20(5):576-585. Oct., 1936.

43. Lorimer, Frank, and Frederick Osborn. The dynamics of population. New York, 1934.

44. McKain, W. C., jr., and C. A. Anderson. "Assortative mating." Sociology and Social Research 21(5):411-418. May-June, 1937.

45. Malzburg, Benjamin. "Marital studies in relation to the prevalence of mental diseases." Psychiatric Quarterly 10:245-261. April, 1936.

46. Margold, Charles W. "Is legal marriage losing ground?" Journal of Social Hygiene 21(7/8/9):391-3. Oct.-Nov.-Dec., 1935.

47. Patterson, S. Howard. "Family desertion and non-support, II." Journal of Delinquency 7:299-333. Nov., 1922.

48. Perkins, H. F. "Adoption and fertility." Eugenical News 21 (5): 95-101. Sept.-Oct., 1936.

49. Petersen, Kenneth M. Early sex information and its influence on later concepts. Unpublished M. A. thesis, College of Education, University of Colorado, 1938.

50. Popenoe, Paul. "Maternal impressions." Journal of Heredity 6:512-518. Nov., 1915.

51. ———. "Long life means many children." Journal of Heredity 7(3):99-100. March, 1916.

52. ———. "Consanguineous marriage." Journal of Heredity 7:343-346. Aug., 1916.

53. ———. "Eugenics and college education." School and Society 6:438-441. Oct. 13, 1917.

54. "Large families." Journal of Heredity 8(7):299-302. July, 1917.

55. ———. "The marriage of kin." Scientific Monthly 17(5):427-434. Nov., 1923.

56. ———. "Some eugenic aspects of illegitimacy." Journal of Social Hygiene 9:513-527. Dec., 1923.

57. ———. Modern Marriage: a handbook for men. (First edition). New York, 1925.

58. ———. Problems of human reproduction. Baltimore, 1926.

59. ———. The conservation of the family. Baltimore, 1926.

60. ———. "Early marriage and happiness." Journal of Social Hygiene 12(9):544-549. Dec., 1926.

61. ———. "Marriage rate among nurses." Eugenical News 12(1):8. Jan., 1927.

62. ———. "Eugenic sterilization in California. 6. Marriage rates of the psychotic." Journal of Nervous and Mental Diseases 68(1):17-27. July, 1928.

63. ———. "Eugenic sterilization in California. 8. Menstruation and salpingectomy among the feebleminded." Pedagogical Seminary and Journal of Genetic Psychology 35:303-311. 1928.

64. ———. "The extent of mental diseases and defect in the American population." Journal of Juvenile Research 13(2):97-103. 1929.

65. ———. "Some effects of a state law requiring delay before a marriage license is issued." Journal of Social Hygiene 15(8):449-456. Nov., 1929.

66. ———. The child's heredity. Baltimore, 1929.

67. ———. Practical applications of heredity. Baltimore, 1930.

68. ———. "Eugenical sterilization in California. 19. A statistical study of the patients of a psychiatrist in private practice." American Journal of Psychiatry 10(1):117-133. July, 1930.

69. ———. Collected papers on eugenic sterilization in California. Human Betterment Foundation, Pasadena, 1930.

70. ———. "How can colleges prepare their students for marriage and parenthood?" Journal of Home Economics 22(3):169-178. Mar., 1930.

71. ———. "Feeblemindness today." Journal of Heredity 21(10):421-431. Oct., 1930.

72. ———. "A family consultation service." Journal of Social Hygiene 17:309-322. 1931.

73. ———. "Heredity and mental deficiency." Mental Hygiene 15(3):570-575. July, 1931.

74. ———. "Marriage counselling," in A decade of progress in eugenics. Baltimore, 1932.

75. ———. "How can young people get acquainted?" Journal of Social Hygiene 18(4): 218-224. Apl., 1932.

76. ———. "Can the family have two heads?" Sociology and Social Research 18:12-17. 1933.

77. ———. "Divorce and remarriage from a eugenic point of view." Social Forces 12(1):48-50. Oct., 1933.

78. ———. "Social life for high school boys and girls." Journal of Social Hygiene 20(5):244-248. May, 1934.

79. ———. "Cooperation in family relations." Journal of Home Economics 26(8):482-486. Oct., 134.

80. ———. "Betrothal." Journal of Social Hygiene 22(9): 442-448. Dec., 1934.

81. ———. "Divorce as a biologist views it." Marriage Hygiene, Feb., 1935.

82. ———. "Castration et stérilization." Rapport présenté au troisième section du Congrès Pénal et Pénitentiaire International. Berlin, 1935.

83. ———. "The proportion of civil marriages." Journal of Social Hygiene 21(7/8/9):370. Oct.-Nov.-Dec., 1935.

84. ———. "Where are the marriageable men?" Social Forces 14(2):257-262. Dec., 1935.

85. ———. "The fertility of divorcees." Journal of Heredity 27(4):166-168. Apl., 1936.

86. ———. "Motivation of childless marriages." Journal of Heredity 27(12):469-472. Dec., 1936.

87. ———. "Marital counselling with special reference to frigidity." Western Journal of Surgery, Obstetrics, and Gynecology. Jan., 1937.

88. ———. "Assortative mating for occupational level." Journal of Social Psychology 8:270-274. May, 1937.

89. ———. "Mate selection." American Sociological Review 2(5):735-743. Oct., 1937.

90. ———. "Can we afford children?" Forum 98:315-318. Dec., 1937.

91. ———. "Intelligence, heredity, and selection." Journal of Heredity 29(2):61-62. Feb., 1938.

92. ———. "A study of 738 elopements." American Sociological Review 3(1):47-48. Feb., 1938.

93. ———. "Heredity and education." Ohio Journal of Science 38(4):207-210. July, 1938.

94. ———. "Success of civil and religious marriages." Eugenical News 23(4):70-71. July-Aug., 1938.

95. ———. "Remarriage of divorcees to each other." American Sociological Review 3(5):695-699. Oct., 1938.

96. ———. "A college education for marriage." Journal of Social Hygiene 25(4):(1-6). Apl., 1939.

97. ——— and Roswell Hill Johnson. Applied eugenics (first edition). New York, 1918.

98. ———. Applied eugenics (revised edition). New York, 1933.

99. ——— and E. S. Gosney. Twenty-eight years of sterilization in California. Human Betterment Foundation, Pasadena, 1937.

100. ——— and Donna Wicks Neptune. "Marital happiness in two generations." Mental Hygiene 21(2):218-223. Apl., 1937.

101. ———. "Acquaintance and betrothal." Social Forces 16(4):(1-4). May, 1938.

102. Price, Bronson. "Homogamy and the intercorrelation of capacity traits." Annals of Eugenics 7(1):22-27. 1936.

103. Sait, Una B. New horizons for the family. N. Y., 1938.

104. Sapir, Edward. "Observations on the sex problem in America." American Journal of Psychiatry 8(3):519-534. Nov., 1928.

105. Schroeder, Clarence Wesley, of the University of Chicago; study in Peoria, Ill., quoted by Associated Press, March, 5, 1939.

106. Stix, Regine K., and Dorothy G. Wiehl. "Abortion and the public health." American Journal of Public Health 28(5):621-628. May, 1938.

107. Symonds, Percival M. "Sex differences in the life problems and interests of adolescents." School and Society 43(11-18):751-2. May 30, 1936.

108. Terman, Lewis M., et al. Psychological factors in marital happiness. New York, 1938.

109. ——— and Winifred B. Johnson. "Methodology and results of recent studies in marital adjustment." American Sociological Review 4(3):307-324. June, 1939.

110. ——— and Catherine Cox Miles. Sex and personality. New York, 1937.

111. Thomas, Dorothy Swain. Social aspects of the business cycle. London, 1925.

112. Unsigned. "The survival of families." Metropolitan Life Ins. Co. Statistical Bulletin 12(4):3-5. Apl., 1931.

113. ———. "Whom do the widowed and divorced marry?" Metropolitan Life Ins. Co. Statistical Bulletin 17(12):3-5. Dec., 1936.

114. ———. "Marriage and long life." Metropolitan Life Ins. Co. Statistical Bulletin 18(2):7-10. Feb., 1937.

115. ———. "Ages of brides and grooms." Metropolitan Life Ins. Co. Statistical Bulletin 18(5):5-8. May, 1937.

116. ———. "The marriage rate and the business cycle." Metropolitan Life Ins. Co. Statistical Bulletin 19(7):1-3. July, 1938.

117. ———. "June brides and other brides." Metropolitan Life Ins. Co. Statistical Bulletin 19(9):1-3. Sept., 1938.

118. ———. "Age at marriage and remarriage." Metropolitan Life Ins. Co. Stat. Bull. 20(4):4-5. Apl., 1939.

119. ———. "The marriage rate in wartime." Metropolitan Life Ins. Co. Statistical Bulletin 20(11):4-6. Nov., 1939.

120. Unwin, J. D. Sex and culture. London, 1934.

121. Waldstein, Martha G. "A maternal health center reviews its patients." Journal of Contraception 4(9):203-209. Nov., 1939.

122. Waller, Willard. The old love and the new; divorce and readjustment. New York, 1930.

123. ———. The family, a dynamic interpretation. New York, 1938.

124. Watson, Goodwin B. "Happiness among adult students of education." Journal of Educational Psychology 21: 79-109. 1930.

125. Whelpton, P. K., and Nelle E. Jackson. "Prolificacy distribution of white wives." Population Index 5(3):146-148. July, 1939.

126. Wile, Ira S. "Mental disorder as a factor in divorce." Eugenical News 23(5):81-92. Sept.-Oct., 1938.

127. Willoughby, Raymond R. "A scale of emotional maturity." Journal of Social Psychology 3(3). 1932.

128. ———. "Fertility and intelligence of college men." Science 87:86-87. 1938.

129. Woodhouse, Chase Going. "A study of 250 successful families." Social Forces 8:511-532. 1930.

130. ———. "Managing the money in successful families." Journal of Home Economics 23(1):(1-8). Jan., 1931.

131. Woods, Frederick Adams. "Successful men have larger families." Journal of Heredity 19:271-279. 1928.

INDEX

293